MY MENTAL REVIVAL

Understanding and Receiving Freedom from Mental and Emotional Abuse from a Christian Worldview

Ryan O'Connell

ISBN 979-8-89309-215-8 (Paperback)
ISBN 979-8-89309-217-2 (Hardcover)
ISBN 979-8-89309-216-5 (Digital)

Covenant Books
11661 Hwy 707
Murrells Inlet, SC 29576
www.covenantbooks.com

CONTENTS

PROLOGUE

Your First Two Steps

If you have picked up this book, it is because you have either been the victim of or know someone who has been the victim of mental and or emotional abuse. It should be understood that this book is by no means a substitute for therapy, and it is recommended that this resource only be used in conjunction with other materials to help break free from the grip of mental and/or emotional abuse.

It should also be understood that the material within this book is written through the eyes of a survivor with a Christian worldview. Therefore, many recommendations found within the pages of this book are founded upon Christian values and the use of the Bible.

If you are still reading this, it means that you are open to any and all options in overcoming your mental or emotional abuse. I want to congratulate you on taking the first step into your freedom from a mentally or emotionally abusive relationship. This is where your journey to wholeness begins, and I look forward to seeing you at the end of this journey being free and able to live with purpose, just as God has intended for you. Try to think back before the relationship with your abuser began. You were lighthearted, always had a smile on your face. You had contentment and joy in your life, but it's been so long since you've experienced those emotions. Then you met them, the person that would change your life forever. You had so much innocence to the world of mental pain and anguish, but it has become as normal to you now, as if you were a child carrying a security blanket. The emotional torment you experience has become your ever-present friend, yet you hold on to the person responsible for making you feel this way. It goes beyond that though. Not only do you remain in the relationship with the person who makes you feel the way that you do, but you are terrified to lose them, as if your world will somehow lose all meaning if you were to lose that person. After all, how could someone who you love so much possibly be the root cause of your pain? And within that question, we also find the answer. How could someone that *you* love—notice there is no mention of love coming from the other person to you, rather there is unconditional love given by you to another person—in most cases, give nothing in return.

Before you angrily close this book and desire to defend the abusive party, let me ask you this: What was the last caring gesture that your significant other performed for you? When was the last time that your abuser sacrificed themselves in an attempt to make you feel happy? If you have trouble answering these questions, perhaps you should continue to read on. And if you are still angry but realize that there is some truth to these questions, then let me congratulate you a second time. You have now taken your second step into getting free from mental and emotional abuse. That step is the step of recognizing the abuse. Choosing to acknowledge that there has been some form of mental or emotional abuse, which you have experienced, is the key to unlocking the doors in your heart and mind, which will allow you to walk into freedom.

The question that you must answer for yourself is, are you ready to be free of mental and emotional abuse in your life? This requires a great deal of introspection and strength to view the other person as they really are. Most victims of abuse will always attempt to defend and excuse their abusers, but through the pages of this book, you will come to find that the person you believed you loved was a facade, that you were never truly awful to the other person. As a matter of fact, the only thing you were guilty of in the relationship was loving another human being unconditionally and, finally, that you were never going to be able to make your abuser happy but that you can be truly happy, even after the ending of an abusive relationship.

The truths found within this book are intended to help abuse victims get their lives back and begin to live with freedom and purpose. For all those that have been victims of mental and emotional abuse, I am sincerely sorry for your pain. It is not fair what was done to you or how you were treated, but know this: You still have value, and you are greatly loved. I believe in you, and I know that there is something better out there for you. If you are ready, fasten your seat belt because you are getting ready to launch out into an awesome adventure in which you will see the old you seemingly be resurrected, you will experience joy and peace in your life once again, and you will know freedom from your current torment. It will not be easy to hear some of the truths this book has to offer, and some of them may leave you angry and furious. We will discuss how to handle those emotions of anger and frustration in a later chapter, but for now, let's simply take the next step in our healing journey. What is the next step?—understanding what just happened to you.

PART 1

Just the Facts

CHAPTER 1

What Just Happened?

It starts out as a pretty normal Friday night. You and your friends have all bought tickets for the newest Marvel movie, and you are ecstatic! Not only is the movie supposed to be incredible, but you've heard that there is a teaser in the end credits that leaks information about the next release that Marvel is preparing to put out. You arrive to the movies early to ensure that you get your tickets and concessions with plenty of time to rush in and find quality seats before the movie starts! As you're waiting in line, you hear a familiar voice call your name. It's one of your friends from work that you had planned on coming to see the movie with, but who is that person with them? You've never been a believer of love at first sight, but there seems to be something about this person that draws your attention. As you are introduced, you can't help but feel that there is some sort of mysterious chemistry between the two of you. You strike up conversation with this new mystery person, and the conversation continues from the ticket line to the concessions line, into the theater, and even into the opening advertisements and trailers for upcoming movies, which is usually one of your favorite parts of going to the movies. The movie starts, and all you can think about throughout the entire movie is that you have to get their contact information. You find it hard to focus on the movie and find yourself feeling nervous and anxious about asking the other person for their cell number. Finally, the movie ends, and as you leave, you exchange contact info with the person that you have met that evening. You think to yourself, *I must be the luckiest person in the world! Why would they be willing to communicate with me?* You begin texting back and forth, and everything seems to be clicking. They respond enthusiastically and quickly from the messages that you send them, and you feel like you are the most important person in the world to them. They come to you with their problems and complaints and leave you feeling like the hero that they've always needed. You now feel that your life has a purpose: to make this person happy and to be their hero. The person then begins to communicate with you that you both have so much in common. They point out all the things that you like, and to your surprise, they are all things that they like as well. Everything about this person is everything that you have ever dreamed of, and you can hardly believe how lucky you are to have found them. Eventually, the texting leads into flirting, which is met with flirting in return. And before you know it, you are now dating this person that was a total stranger to you. The only problem is that the relationship developed entirely too quickly and was based upon surface-area qualities, which could be shared by any two human beings.

There are stages in the mental and emotional abuse cycle, which are completely controlled by the abuser. The above-described cycle is what is known as the idealization stage. In this stage, the abuser creates the ideal relationship from your perspective, as well as the perspective of all onlookers into the relationship. There is often love bombing, pictures taken together, and constant flattery and flirting that takes place. You are made to believe that this individual was miserable with their life until you came along, that is. You are their only place of contentment, and you are the only person or thing in this world, which can make them truly happy.

First, from a biblical worldview, this is a huge red flag. The Bible says, "Dear friends, since God so loved us, we also ought to love one another. No one has ever seen God; but if we love one another, God lives in us and his love is made complete in us" (1 John 4:11–12).

Anyone who claims to be a Christian should have God's love made complete in them. If this is true, then how could they reveal to you how victimized they have been and that you are the only person or thing that can bring them true happiness and contentment? If they have truly experienced the love and presence of God in their lives, then the place where they should be able to find true joy and contentment is in relationship with God through the blood of Jesus.

Nonetheless, you buy into every word, and what's worse, you desire and begin to crave the feeling of being needed in order to produce happiness for this person. Your life at this point has developed a new purpose: to bring joy and contentment to this other person. No longer are you the happy-go-lucky person that had been so excited about going to the movies with your friends three Friday nights ago, but now you seem to always be uptight. Your friends and family mention to you that you don't quite seem to be the same person you were before you started dating this other person. You begin to lash out at the people that used to mean so much to you, but you don't notice or recognize it because your thoughts are constantly fixed on your significant other and ways in which you can make them happy. It is not your job and has never been your job to make another person feel fulfilled. That is the job of God. And if you begin to try to fill His role in that person's life, you are venturing into dangerous territory because you are only human and cannot play the part of a perfect God. Eventually, as hard as you may try, you will fail the other person. The Bible says in Psalm 118:8, "It is better to take refuge in the Lord, Than to trust in man."

There is no set time frame for the idealization stage from beginning to end, but it often does not last long, as the victim of the mental and emotional abuse is often reeled in by the deceivingly innocent outer expressions of the abuser. You are led to believe that you are a godsent gift to this person to help keep them safe and to fulfill the abuser's every whim in an attempt to keep their attention. After all, you were the lucky one to find such a beautiful person, who also calls themselves a Christian, and you two seem to have so much in common together. You begin to fantasize and consider your long-term future with this person, and they express the same thing to you. You begin to think to yourself that this is simply too good to be true, and unfortunately, you're right because the second stage of the mental and emotional abuse cycle is getting ready to begin: the devaluation stage.

The devaluation stage of the mental and emotional abuse cycle begins with the abuser beginning to neglect the victim inside of the relationship. All of a sudden, the "good morning" and "good night" texts begin to dwindle and eventually are no more. You express your disappointment at the change in your relationship, and it is met with frustration and anger on the part of the abuser. Rather than trying to understand your feelings and help you to work through them, the abuser uses them as fuel for the abuse to increase. They begin to accuse you of being clingy or needy and insinuate that your feelings have no space inside the relationship. They may say something similar to "just because your feelings are real doesn't mean that they are true." This downplay of your emotions may seem like an attempt to comfort, but the truth is that this is nothing more than the abuser revealing to the victim that their feelings truly do not matter. But how could this be? Everything seemed to be going great, and then there was a total 180. It does not make sense to you because you do not suffer from NPD. The trigger can switch in a matter of seconds, and it leaves the victim reeling. The emotional whiplash alone is enough to make the victim wonder what they have done to cause this type of reaction in their significant other. The problem is that these actions are not reactionary based on actions, which the victim has taken, but rather carefully made decisions, which the abuser has put into play. It is not a matter of the victim having unintentionally provoked the abuser but a matter of the abuser deliberately choosing not to care about the feelings of their significant other or how their actions will affect them. At this point, the victim will try to discover what happened, asking their significant other if everything is all right and checking more regularly to see if everything is okay. Rather than a normal response in reassuring the victim and showing genuine care for how they are feeling, the victim will meet these inquiries with aggravation and attacks on the victim's self-esteem, informing them that they are being clingy, needy, or jealous. This only leads to more confusion for the victim of the narcissist because they begin to think that their responses to the abuser's behavior is the problem rather than the behavior of the abuser. The victim will find themselves spinning, trying to figure out exactly what they did wrong and will then begin to bottle up their emotions. This is only the start of the devaluation stage, however, because the abuser will never truly be happy until the victim is completely destroyed. Once the abuser has taken this step into the devaluation stage, it is only a matter of time before they begin to show others the same level of care and adoration they once reserved for you. You will find them frequently talking with the opposite sex and seeking the adoration of others rather than being content with the adoration which you provide. This then leads the victim to feelings of inadequacy and feeling that they are not good enough. The victim finds themselves scrambling. Trying to do anything and everything they possibly can to try to please the abusive person in the relationship. Every attempt to please the abuser is met with mockery and malcontent. Oftentimes, the abuser will have discovered the victim's weaknesses by this time and will begin to unashamedly attack the victim's weaknesses. This will often be done under the guise of humor, but there is nothing funny about this. The victim is left feeling helpless to defend themselves and will begin to doubt their own self-worth. The vicious attacks on the part of the abuser are merciless and relentless and leave the victim starved for love and respect. The victim still has hopes and believes that they are the only person that can possibly make their abuser happy, and their purpose for their lives must be fulfilled. Threats begin to be made by the abuser to leave and move on with their lives. This throws even more chaos into the mind and heart of the victim. By this time, the abuser likely has already selected their next target and are only stringing the current victim along long enough to see them be completely destroyed.

This leads to a serious question, which all abuse victims face. Why me? You must understand that your abuser did not select you because you were weak and easy to control. Rather, your abuser selected you because they saw your strengths. You are a kind, loving, and caring person, and you should never feel ashamed of those qualities. They are strong and profound and serve as great tools to many people's lives. These very same tools that you spent years developing are exactly what your abuser found so desirable about you. Not being capable of empathy but craving the attention of someone, the abuser will look for only the most successful victims. The problem for the abuser is that any person who has worked so hard to build themselves will never willingly accept abusive behavior. This is why the idealization stage is the first and most important stage of the mental and emotional abuse cycle. The abuser must get you to believe that they are treating the way that you deserve to be treated. Once they have gotten you to lower your guard, they will then begin to step into the devaluation stage. Now that you know why you were selected by the abuser, you must understand that the abuser's attention was only ever to destroy you. This is the exact opposite of what happens in a normal and healthy relationship. Think about it. During the entire abusive relationship, all that you ever did was try to build up your abuser and make them feel loved. You encouraged them to live out their dreams, backed up and supported them, and showed them love, loyalty, and respect. Now, in healthy relationships, the reaction of a person to this type of treatment would be to give the same love, loyalty, and respect to the person that has already extended it but not so in the mentally and emotionally abusive relationship. The feeling of never being good enough and always needing to do more for the abuser becomes the burning passion for the victim. It is driven by fear and feeling that they need the abuser in their lives in order for their lives to have any sort of meaning. This then is responded to by mediocre treatment at best and abusive and downplaying language and actions at the very worst. It should be noted that the abuser will likely bounce back and forth between the idealization stage and devaluation stage regularly. This keeps the victim guessing and ensures that the abuser always maintains control. One thing to keep in mind about a mental and emotional abuser is that they are always bored and always looking for their next victim. Any member of the opposite sex that is willing to give them a significant amount of time or attention becomes a prime opportunity for the abuser. Once the devaluation stage has begun, and the abuser has selected their next target, it is time for the third and final stage of the mental and emotional abuse cycle: discarding the victim.

Discarding the victim is by far the most draining and painful of the stages of the mentally and emotionally abusive relationship because this is not your normal breakup. Whereas most people after a relationship have ended just want to be left alone by the other party or desire to cultivate a friendship instead with the other person, the mental and emotional abuser seeks to completely destroy the life of the victim. It is not enough to simply part ways because the abuser still desires the attention of the victim. While they may not want the victim, they don't want anyone else to have them either, and they certainly don't want to see the victim happy or moving forward with their lives. This stage of the mental and emotional abuse process often includes the bringing in of a new victim. For the victim, the thoughts that swirl in their mind are, *Was I not good enough? What does this person have that I don't? What is wrong with me?* We will touch on this subject a little later, but oftentimes, this is the reason why the victim often asks themselves upon researching the narcissistic tendencies if they are or were the narcissist. This is a cycle where truth will set in. And immediately following the feeling of liberation from an abusive partner, the feeling of doubt will begin to make the victim feel that perhaps they were the abusive partner in the relationship. Why would this not be true? After all, the abuser has placed in your mind for an extended period of time that you were the source of all issues in the relationship. It is only natural for your mind to go back to what you had believed to be true for such a prolonged period of time. However, this is hopeful information because if you were truly the narcissist, you wouldn't even allow the thought of you being the narcissistic person to enter your mind because you would not be capable of that kind of self-reflection or inventory. The abuser will be intentional to bring up information that insinuates they are spending time with another person and will pretend to be truly happy with their next victim. This is all a facade, however, because the abuser is incapable of being happy themselves. This is one reason that the abuser desires to destroy the victim because they are incapable of their own happiness and therefore do not want to see it in other people. Ironically, this was most likely another of your desirable traits that attracted the abuser to you. Think back to before the abuse;

were you a genuinely happy person? If you answered yes to this question, don't fret; you are not alone, and you will return to that happy state of living once again. It will take time and often need to go zero contact with the abuser in order for you to return to your normal state. But it is possible, and the journey is so worth it.

CHAPTER 2

Why?

It is one of the first questions we learn as children. For anyone who has children of their own, you can understand the frustrations that can come with this inquisitive and often repetitive one-word question: Why? For the victim of mental and emotional abuse, the question rings true and ends in many different ways. Why didn't I try harder? Why wasn't I enough? Why did they do this to me? Why couldn't I see past their lies? These are all fair questions. But they all come back to the same one-word question: Why? This question leads us to the next step that we must take in our walk to freedom from mental and emotional abuse. The next step after taking inventory of what has happened to us is beginning to understand the thought process of the abuser. Now this may seem counterintuitive and feel as if excuses are being made for the abuser. This is not the case, however. Rather, this is a key step to us being able to realize further that none of what happened to us was our fault. Once again, the only thing you were guilty of as the victim is loving someone unconditionally. You will hear those words repeated continually throughout this book because you must retrain your mind to believe and know that you are truly a good person. Gaslighting and half-truths have been told to you so that eventually you begin to question what was real and what was fabricated, and you even begin to doubt yourself being a good person. This is the way that the abuser maintains control over their victims.

Before we go any further, let's take time to take inventory on some of the abusers' typical characteristics. One characteristic of people who suffer from NPD is that they truly are not happy. They are not happy persons because they are incapable of taking self-inventory and discovering who they truly are. This in itself is a red flag because the Bible itself discusses in Romans 12:3 how it is that we are to view ourselves and how we are supposed to judge, whether or not we are good persons. Romans 12:3 reads, "For by the grace given me I say to every one of you: Do not think of yourself more highly than you ought, but rather think of yourself with sober judgment, in accordance with the faith God has distributed to each of you."

In other words, this portion of scripture is instructing us to check our internal persons. This should not be a onetime thing but rather a way in which we conduct ourselves daily so that we can be sure that we are building ourselves and others up and helping to build the kingdom of God. Unfortunately, as stated before, the narcissistic person is incapable of this level of self-reflection. If they were capable of doing so, there would be much fewer victims of mental and emotional abuse, and there would be no reason for this book or this adventure to self-healing you find yourself on. Most people are capable of looking into themselves and seeing ways that they could have operated differently in different situations, which would not harm the people they care about. For the person suffering from NPD however, this is not an option. They likely have been trained since childhood to put up a front that makes them appear to be perfect, and this stunts the growth of the person. Since the abuser is incapable of introspection, they often try to fix up the outside to look perfect. They try to make it appear that they have all their ducks in a row and that they are much so okay. Often, they will be in constant want of new items—clothes, vehicles, homes, etc.—all for the sake of maintaining a certain appearance and perhaps in search of true happiness. It is very sad because while excitement and adrenaline may carry them for a short period, they are never truly fulfilled because after the shine wears off or the clothes have been seen more than once or the new vehicle has been driven for a prolonged period of time, the person finds themselves back in the same old trap of constantly trying to pursue happiness and contentment but never being able to attain it.

You may be wondering if this is in regard to relationships as well, and the overwhelming answer is yes. A person who suffers from NPD will even become bored in their relationships and begin to chase something younger, older, more built, funnier, more intelligent, wealthier, etc. in the eyes of the abuser. However, they are never truly fulfilled. After a short stint with person after person after person, the abuser will find themselves bored and begin to seek yet another victim. While it may be sad for each person who falls victim to the narcissist's behavior, it is even sadder still for the abuser themselves. How miserable it must be to live a life in which you are constantly searching for happiness but unable to find it. If we are to be honest however, we might begin doing introspection and thinking to ourselves, *I don't feel happy or content myself.* You are correct. You currently are not happy or content in yourself. As a matter of fact, it has probably been a while since you have been unashamedly happy and content in your current situation. Who could blame you for feeling that way? Ever since the devaluation stage set in, all you have been told is the wrong that you have done, how you have come up short, and ways that you need to improve or change yourself. How ironic that the very people who should be taking self-inventory are the ones informing real people of changes that they should make on the outside.

It is sad and a real shame that the outward appearance matters more to the abuser than a genuine person who genuinely cares about them. You are a real person with real feelings, and more than likely, you made whatever changes necessary to your outward appearance in an attempt to make your abuser happy. Since you have been told for so long that you are coming up short all across the relationship, it is no wonder that you experience false feelings and doubts that your abuser has placed inside of you. If you can, try to think back to a time where you did feel happy and content. Oddly enough, you were probably single and enjoying your life. This was probably also prior to your relationship with your abuser. What exactly does this mean? It means that rather than lifting your abuser up, your abuser effectively brought you down. This was because you spent so much time and energy trying to make the other person happy. You began to neglect friendships and other important relationships in your life all for the sake of your abuser. In doing this, you even began to forget about what made you happy.

We will discuss rediscovering your true self in another chapter, but for now, let's get back to the thought process of the abuser. Essentially, what has taken place is that you have projected pieces of yourself onto each other. In the case of the abuser, they have projected their feelings of unhappiness, self-doubt, and desire for no introspection onto you. No doubt, you were always busy running around in some way while in your relationship with your abuser. This is because the abuser is always bored, and they detest and despise time spent alone. Left only with themselves and their own personal thoughts, they keep themselves busy scrolling through social media, texting others, or in some other way, attempting to distract themselves from doing any introspection. Most normal people appreciate time alone, and it can even be therapeutic at points, not so for the person suffering from NPD. They will do whatever they can to keep themselves busy and create opportunities to make sure they don't have to go deep, even with themselves. Going deep would result in the necessity to be open and vulnerable about one's self to one's self. And as discussed earlier, there is no room for openness or vulnerability in the life of the abuser because that would require being honest about who they are. Because they have never taken the time for introspection, the abuser does not know who they truly are. Going into the dark and discovering who they truly are is not an exciting adventure to the narcissistic personality but rather a frightening undertaking to be avoided at all costs. They do not know who they truly are and furthermore do not know how to respond to the truths they may discover. But for a normal person, this is the adventure of a lifetime. Getting to discover who they truly are and what truly makes them happy becomes one of the most exciting parts of their lives because they discover they can find happiness and contentment within themselves without the aid of another person. This book being written from a biblical worldview it should be noted that, for some, the contentment is discovered in discovering who it is that God says they are. This becomes dependent upon a love that is consistent and will never fail, and that is the safest place you can put your trust.

The second characteristic that a person suffering from NPD will display is that they simply are not trustworthy. Now anyone at all will tell you that there cannot be a relationship without trust. This is very true; however, the deceitfulness that comes from a person suffering from NPD comes in many forms. One of the primary forms of dishonesty is gaslighting. This takes place when an abuser causes the victim to believe that they are truly in the wrong for whatever argument may be taking place between the abuser and victim. Unfortunately, the level of deception that the abuser is capable of far exceeds the victim's capability to combat it. The Bible discusses this topic as well:

> One who is faithful in a very little is also
> faithful in much, and one who is dishonest in a
> very little is also dishonest in much. (Luke 16:10)

Please do not confuse not being trustworthy with being a chronic liar. While some abusers may be in the habit of regularly lying to their significant other, it is more common for them to simply withhold information. While part of the truth may be spoken by the abuser, there is always a glaring fact that would be held back from the audience of the narcissist. As discussed earlier, the abuser is incapable of introspection and therefore will do anything to protect themselves from the truth coming out. They may ask you, "Please, don't destroy my name." All the while, they are going to great lengths to try to destroy you completely. This is because the abuser's half-truths are built from a house of cards. They do not desire the truth, only enough for their victim to come off as the abusive person. And if the truth begins to be exposed, or there is potential for it to be exposed, the abuser becomes angry and lashes out at the victim. Since the abuser is not trustworthy, it only makes sense that they would become angry when approached with the truth. Most people will not become angry when faced with the truth; they will become angry when they feel that they have been deceived or lied to. Unfortunately, the abused person has often experienced so much damage by the abuser that they listen to the abuser's justifications for their deception and accept them, once again, taking responsibility for their response to the abuser's deceptive and morally wrong behaviors rather than the abuser being held responsible for their behaviors, which prompted the response of the victim. This in itself is a form of deception because the victim is led to believe that there is something wrong with them expressing their feelings. Slowly but surely, the victim becomes so tired of fighting that they begin to bury how they're really feeling, and the abuser takes full control of their victim's emotional health. Now that the victim has lost their voice in expressing how the abuser's actions make them feel, the abuser is free to live how they want and do whatever will make them happy in the moment without having to be bothered with the feelings of another person. Now, from an outsider's perspective, this would be a clear red flag that the abuser does not care about the feelings of the other person. This leads us to the third characteristic of the abuser.

The third characteristic that people suffering from NPD share is that they are incapable of empathy. They are not able to place themselves into the other person's shoes and consider how their actions may be making another person feel. This often leads back to the first characteristic of a person suffering from NPD, which was that they are not happy people. Since they are incapable of making themselves happy, since they are unhappy, they do not understand that their actions and words also have an effect on other people. Their constant pursuit for their own happiness, which undoubtedly goes unfulfilled time and again, ultimately results in the harming of other people emotionally because they do not care who they may harm, so long as they may experience a moment of their own happiness. Once the moment is over, however, the abuser is left with damage control that must be done. And instead of taking responsibility for their actions, the abuser will lash out at their current victim and begin to discredit their feelings and opinions without apology. In Matthew 22:37–40 the Bible says, "Jesus replied: 'Love the Lord your God with all your heart and with all your soul and with all your mind.' This is the first and greatest commandment. And the second is like it: 'Love your neighbor as yourself.' All the Law and the Prophets hang on these two commandments."

Right here, Jesus approaches the entire issue of the person suffering from NPD. We are instructed to love God and then to love others as ourselves. The last half of this statement has a conundrum built right within itself. The abuser in the relationship is not capable of self-reflection and therefore is not capable of true self-love. If this is the case, how can a person possibly love their neighbors if they are not first capable of loving themselves? Unfortunately, there are many victims who have suffered from a lack of empathy in their lives. Because of this lack of empathy, rather than the victim's cries for help being heard, they are silenced by the abuser. In most situations, the relationship a victim will find themselves in will be that of a trophy for their abuser. Time alone with the victim is not a necessity because the abuser has already trapped the attention of the victim. The abuser will often ask to hang out in groups and surround themselves with people they find attractive and can flirt with. This is where the double standard for the abuser will set in because the victim is expected by the abuser to give no attention or energy to any other person in the room, whereas the abuser has full permissions to go and sit with whoever they like and even flirt without any repercussions. Once again, the feelings of the victim do not matter as long as the abuser feels happy in the moment. This lack of empathy, however, goes beyond their relationship with their significant other. There will often be squabbles and problems between the abuser and others within their friend groups as the abuser will not take into consideration their friend's feelings in any particular situation either. This frees the abuser from any and all responsibilities to anyone and anything but their own happiness. And since the person suffering from NPD is naturally unhappy in and of themselves, there are no limits as to how far the abusive party will go to chase even a moment's happiness.

One of the first things that an abuser will say is that they hate drama, yet drama appears to be all that surrounds this person. They are incapable of feeling content because of their inability to see and accept themselves for who they truly are. If this is true, and the abuser is incapable of loving themselves, then how can they possibly love another person? It should also be noted that the abuser cannot receive love the way that they should be able to because they do not believe they are worthy of love. By this, it does not mean they do not believe they do not deserve love, but rather they do not understand who they are and that they are worthy of love because of who they are. The truth is that every single person on earth deserves to be loved and cared for. In simply being born, each person is unique and deserves to be the recipient of love. After all, at our very core, each person has an inborn desire to be accepted exactly as they are. For the individual suffering from NPD, they do not believe that they will be accepted for who they are, so they take on good characteristics of others around them in hopes that they will be accepted for those characteristics. But these false characteristics cannot last forever because they are not core values of the abuser. It is at the taking off of these false characteristics that the transition from the idealization stage to the devaluation stage transpires. Because the core values and beliefs of the victim are not true core values and beliefs of the abuser, it is not uncommon for the victim to begin to compromise on their core values and beliefs. This leaves the victim feeling a great sense of remorse and guilt for their actions as they have developed a sense of pride in having boundaries they are unwilling to cross. Any attempt to express these feelings to the abuser, however, is met with anger and blame shifting, claiming that the victim was fully to blame for the deconstruction of their own values and even insinuating that they would never have crossed the line if the victim had not initiated first. Rather than expressing empathy and trying to comfort the victim, the abuser places full blame on the victim for the compromises that have taken place. As a reminder, the person suffering from NPD is incapable of placing themselves into the other person's shoes. The feelings and emotions that other people express are not to be tolerated, especially when they interfere with the abuser's pursuit of happiness. They do not care about how they make another person feel because they are incapable of considering the feelings of the other person involved.

We started off this chapter with a rather simple question: Why? It is my hope that you understand that what has happened to you was not because you were not a good person or that you treated the other person poorly. Rather, the reason you are experiencing so much pain and backlash now is because your abuser was suffering from a very real mental disorder, which caused them to not be happy in themselves, not be trustworthy or honest with you, and to be incapable of considering your feelings when making decisions and performing actions during the time of your relationship. In no way does this make you inadequate or unworthy of love. Your value has not been lessened as the result of this mentally and emotionally abusive relationship. Rather, your value has been raised to a much higher level because you were a person who found themselves in an impossible situation and still fought for the person you thought that your abuser really was. This does not make you a failure; this makes you someone that loved unconditionally, and that will carry you far once you have moved on and find yourself in a healthy relationship.

CHAPTER 3

If It Wasn't Real, Then Why Does This Hurt?

Now that we have an understanding of the mindset of the abuser, it is time to look deeper into the hurt that you have experienced. This is one of the hardest things that an abuse victim will ever have to experience because it is a matter of reopening the wound. No one likes to revisit a point of time or location in their lives when they have experienced pain. Most individuals who have been a part of a major car accident have great difficulty in driving again and, even when they do, will avoid the scene of the accident at all costs. However, please understand that knowing the why behind the pain is just as important as getting past it. It is not enough to say that your abuser was a narcissist and move on with your life because there is no closure in that. The unfortunate thing about the person suffering from NPD is that they will never admit or be willing to consider that they might be a narcissist. Because of this, approaching and confronting the narcissistic person simply is not an option as the conversation will only end in denial and rejection of the truth and subtle gaslighting. Therefore, as the victim of abuse, closure must be received in a different way. There will be no apology or attempt to make amends on the part of the abuser as that would require them admitting that they were wrong. The best way that one can receive closure is to discover the truth about what has transpired to them, and then choose to move on, knowing the truth themselves. The question then is, what is the truth? There are different pieces of truth that will help in the process of receiving closure.

The first piece of truth that a victim must understand is that to the narcissistic person, your relationship was not real. Now, how could this be? The love bombing and idealization stage were so real; how could all this have been a facade? It may not make sense, but the truth is that to the person suffering from NPD, none of what transpired in your relationship was real. This can be a very painful truth for the victim to take in because it means that the person that they believe they loved never truly cared about them in return. It indicates to the victim that there must be something wrong with them because the other person did not reciprocate all the love and affection that you gave them. However, you must remember that an abuser is not a normal person. Under normal circumstances, for a person not to respond in kind with love for love will bother both parties. Often, there is not a mutual attraction, or there is some sort of emotional disconnect between the two parties. However, in the same situation with a narcissistic person, the narcissist is only concerned with their feelings. The victim then pours out lavish amounts of love and is thrilled to receive mediocre treatment in return. This is a very sad state of affairs because the victim is willing to go to any lengths to try to make the abuser happy. Meanwhile, the abusive party is never satisfied and is constantly looking for their next victim. The feelings you experienced during the idealization stage were very real as were your feelings as you entered the devaluation stage. However, none of this was real to your abuser. Because they did not love the victim nor care for the feelings of the victim, the abuser will move on very quickly from whatever relationship they may have had. Fathers will invest time and energy into other kids, boyfriends will find new girlfriends, wives will jump into new relationships, best friends will develop new friendships, and the list goes on. However, in the middle of all this, the victim is left in the dust and debris, begging for life to return to some state of normalcy.

Unfortunately for the victim, everything about the relationship was very real. The victim therefore has difficulty moving on and begins to wonder what is wrong with them. They are left dazed and confused, not understanding what has just happened to them and unable to find any understanding or closure. The reason why the victim is so very confused is because what has just happened to them does not make sense. In a relationship with a normal person, this never would have happened because the normal person is capable of caring about the other person's feelings. Rather than this being a heartbreaking truth for the victim, it should be a shred of light and hope. If it was not real, then there is nothing wrong with you. You are in fact capable of making another person happy and perhaps with much less effort than you gave in your relationship with your abuser. But beyond that, the mediocre treatment you received from your abuser does not have to be what you settle for. You will receive greater love because you are a genuinely loving and caring person. The Bible tells us in Galatians 6:7–9, "Do not be deceived: God cannot be mocked. A man reaps what he sows. Whoever sows to please their flesh, from the flesh will reap destruction; whoever sows to please the Spirit, from the Spirit will reap eternal life."

This is a promise from God, and that is something you can take to the bank. When last I checked, God has never come up short or backed out on His promises. You have sowed love diligently and unsparingly, which means that you will also reap diligent love that is unsparing, and that is a comforting thought.

This then leads us into the second truth in our pursuit of closure that truth is that not only was the relationship not real, but neither was the abuser. What does it mean that the abuser was not real? We discussed earlier in the book about how the abuser does not love themselves. Since they are incapable of self-reflection and therefore self-love, the narcissist cannot reveal who they truly are. When you first met your abuser, everything about them was amazing. You could not believe what you had in common. They were literally like a female version of you. They were literally everything that you had ever wanted or desired. But that quickly changed during the devaluation stage. All of a sudden, everything that drove them wild about you was now a glaring problem. Rather than making you feel like the most special person on earth, you had now become a nuisance to this person that you believed loved you. But how could a person change who they are so quickly? The truth is that you never really met the other person. They determined what you were looking for in a significant other and then made sure that you saw signs of those things in them. You thought that you were attracted to them, but the reality is that all they were doing was mirroring your good qualities in the idealization stage. What was important to you was important to them. But not even a month later, what they said they enjoyed changed drastically, and without you knowing it, you find yourself in a relationship with a different person entirely. The person that you believed you fell in love with did not truly exist. They were simply a mask that your abuser adorned in the idealization phase to ensure that they had your complete and undivided attention. Once they attained their ultimate goal, it was just a matter of time before all the false personality traits they put on to impress you began to disappear. So you see, the person you believed that you loved never truly existed. Whatever it was that attracted you to your abuser was not really a part of who they are. This again can be a bitter pill to swallow for the victim because it only confirms that whatever was between you and your abuser was not real. However, you will come to find that this information is rather freeing than debilitating. This information alone can serve as a confirmation that there was nothing wrong with you throughout the duration of the relationship. Whereas the abuser caused you to believe that any expression of your feelings was in itself innately wrong; the opposite is the actual truth. Not expressing one's feelings in a relationship is not a sign of love on the part of the silent partner but rather a sign of lack of care for the victim on the part of the abuser.

But how can this be true? After all, my abuser told me they loved me. They made me feel like I was the only person capable of making them happy. Yes, and they will do the same exact thing to their next victim. What they portray is not actually who they are because to portray the real them would require self-reflection, followed by admitting who they really are to others around them. And the narcissist we have already discovered is incapable of introspection, let alone openly admitting to others who they really are. Remember, the narcissist must always play the victim. They are not responsible for their own actions and therefore must have a scapegoat to pin the blame on for their selfishness and deceitfulness in the form of gaslighting and leading you to believe that the cause of issues in the relationship is not their self-serving intent but rather your response to their selfish motives and actions, yet throughout the duration of the relationship with your abuser, you loved them unconditionally. Did that not mean anything to them? Was all of the self-sacrifice and servitude that you offered in vain? The unfortunate answer to that question is no. Since the abuser is incapable of feeling happy in and of themselves, the abuser must search for happiness from another source. They are incapable of self-love, and therefore, the expectation is perfection on your part 100 percent of the time. This, of course, is impossible for anyone. Without fail, everyone in your life will let you down at one point or another, whether it is intentional or a mistake, and rest assured that with an abuser, lack of empathy and love in a relationship is never a mistake. It is a cool and calculated decision moment by moment to do what is in their best interest, no matter how it makes others around them feel. With this in mind, it is not a bad thing to try to love the people in your life well. As a matter of fact, we are encouraged to do so. The Bible says in Mark 12:30–31, "Love the Lord your God with all your heart and with all your soul and with all your mind and with all your strength.' The second is this: 'Love your neighbor as yourself.' No other commandment is greater than these."

The person you believed that you fell in love with was not real, therefore all your love and affection was meaningless to the abuser. This is not normal, and eventually you will find someone who is grateful for and returns in kind with the love and affection that you give out so greatly. This is not bad news but rather good news for the victim of mental and emotional abuse because it means that your love is valuable; you were simply peddling it to someone that did not exist.

A third and final truth for victims to be aware of is that the feelings of loss that you are experiencing may be real, but in time you will come to see that they are not warranted. Now this may come off as something a narcissist would be inclined to say, but let's examine this statement versus what an abuser might say. The narcissist will recognize that your feelings have been hurt by saying something like, "Your feelings may be real…" But rather than recognizing the feelings and what might have caused it, the narcissist will instinctually target the feelings and not the behavior, which causes those feelings to be the problem. In the case of our statement "the feelings of loss that you're experiencing may be real…"—can't you hear the empathy in this statement? We choose to recognize the feelings and give them a name and credibility for their existence.

Continuing on, we come to the *but* statement. In the case of the abuser, we will be told, "Your feelings may be real, but they aren't true." This dismisses the feelings of the victim and diminishes that they have any sort of validity to them whatsoever, insinuating that the victim is crazy for feeling the way that they do. However, in our core statement "the feelings of loss that you're experiencing may be real, but in time you will come to see that they are not warranted"— rather than diminishing and making light of the feelings that the victim is experiencing, our statement empowers the victim. Be in your feelings, know them, experience them if this is what you need to ultimately get free of the mental grip and brainwashing you have experienced from your abuser, but know that in time, you will come to realize that those feelings are not valid. Rest assured, you are *not* a bad person. What you were accused of was either not true, or it was viciously blown out of proportion to ensure that you were a bad person. Remember that a narcissist is incapable of taking responsibility for their own actions because this would require introspection. They are only capable of pointing the finger at the response of the victim to their abusive behaviors. What you have done is not wrong, nor does it indicate that there's anything wrong with you as a person. Rather, this shows the true character of your abuser. Know that whatever is happening to you and whatever experience you may be facing in your personal life, God is not mad at you. He loves you and is crazy about you and is still working all things together for your good and His glory. It is easy for the victim of emotional abuse to step into this line of thinking because they are willing to do introspection. And because of the past lies and statements made by the abuser, the victim is left spinning in a world filled with questions and questioning whether they were the abusive person in the relationship or if there was something wrong with how they conducted themselves inside of it. Once again, all that you were guilty of was loving another person whom you believed to be who they said they were. You were honest and forthcoming with your abuser, and often this was only met with feelings of not being good enough. No matter how hard you may have tried, your best was never going to be good enough because your abuser is not happy or content in and of themselves. There will always be another outfit, a newer vehicle, a better house, a more expensive vacation, or any combination of the above among other things that they will need in order to satisfy their constant need to be validated. This is not an issue within yourself but rather a glaring red flag that you missed as a result of being blinded by your genuine and unconditional love for another person. The Bible tells us to "love the Lord your God with all your heart and with all your soul and with all your mind and with all your strength.' The second is this: 'Love your neighbor as yourself.' No other commandment is greater than these" (Jeremiah 17:9).

You may feel that you have lost someone in your life that was truly special, and it is true that you built your abuser up to be this amazing person that you now feel you are missing. For so long, you have justified their ill-treatment to you and accepted mediocre love and care that you now believe that this is normal or even what you deserve. This is completely untrue, especially when walking into a relationship with a person who claims to be a Christian. The truth is that people can only give what they have received. If the love that you received from the other person was anything less than unconditional love, then you deserved better. It may be hard to believe right now, but there is someone out there who is holding on to a love like what you gave to your abuser. They are looking for someone to give it to, just like you are searching for someone to give your love to. One day, your paths will cross, and you will sit there and think to yourself, *How did I settle for so long for so much less than this? How did I determine that I did not deserve this type of treatment in return for the love that I gave to my abuser?* You do deserve unconditional love, just like the love that you gave to your abuser.

One last thought as we conclude this chapter: When you think of how you want to be able to love another person, consider Jesus. He was willing to give you *everything*. I know that it's hard to see your abuser move on and jump from relationship to relationship and victim to next victim. But please be aware that every single relationship they find themselves in will be just as difficult and broken as the one that you found yourself in. But don't shortchange yourself. You may have a burning desire to go and find another person to be with, but don't rush things. Maximize your singleness. Discover the things that you truly enjoy in life. Reestablish your own morals and values. Find what things bother you in a person or are necessary for a relationship to work. Odds are that because of the idealization stage, you overlooked this part of the dating journey with your abuser, and before you knew it, you were so busy trying to make the abuser happy that you fell off to the wayside. Remember, relationships are built on communication and a willingness to compromise. Nobody is going to be a carbon copy of you, so there may be times when you are interested in doing things that your significant other is not, and that is okay. Rather than one party always bowing to the demands of the other, there should be a mutual give-and-take. Spend some time rediscovering the real you. Then when you do meet a person who has some of the same likes and interests that you have, you can develop a friendship with them and determine whether you two would make a good fit or not—all this to say, you are a unique individual, and you deserve to be treated as such. A good litmus test for you moving forward would be, "Does this person make me feel loved in the same way that Jesus loves me?" If the answer is no, or you cannot give an answer, I would say that's a good sign that you deserve better. You are unique, you are loved, and you deserve the very best that another person can offer.

CHAPTER 4

Where Is the Justice?

More than reasonably, as the victim of mental and emotional abuse, you will go through many different emotions during the healing process: feelings of sorrow, loss, and feeling that you are not good enough. However, eventually you will feel the emotion of anger, bitterness, rage, and a demand for justice.

Knowing now what you wish you had known months or even years ago, you experience frustration and wanting to know why everything seems to be going well for your abuser, while things in your life appear to be falling apart. The truth, however, is that unlike your abuser, your entire life needs to be rebuilt. Remember, for the abuser, they have sold you a false product, whereas you have attempted to sell them the genuine article of who you really are. Therefore, the abuser need not completely rebuild their life; they merely change out a mask and move on. For you though, your entire life has been shaken and turned upside down. The person who you thought loved you unconditionally now attacks you unashamedly behind your back, leading others to believe how bad of a person you are. Nothing could be further from the truth because all that you ever did was love and care for the other person unconditionally. Still they point out your flaws and even dig up information from your past from even before you met your abuser. But you have never mentioned anything of your abuser's past or dug into it, so why would your abuser feel the need to dig up information about you? The answer is simple: They cannot be the bad person in the relationship, despite the fact that they are in fact abusive. The fact that the abuser must dig into your past to try to discover information to discredit and smear your name with is a clear red flag of them attempting to cover up something from their own personal life. Rather than taking responsibility for their actions, the abuser must create a world in which they are continuously the victim. This new information leads to great anger and rage and leads you to desire justice. However, know that God will not be mocked. As mentioned in a previous chapter, Galatians 6:7–9 states, "Do not be deceived: God cannot be mocked. A man reaps what he sows. Whoever sows to please their flesh, from the flesh will reap destruction; whoever sows to please the Spirit, from the Spirit will reap eternal life."

It may seem unfair what is happening now, but rest assured that whatever you have sowed, you will also reap. Have you sowed good seed? Did you sow good seed to your abuser? If the answer is yes to both of these questions, then rest assured that good is coming for you as well. Usually, in the beginning stages of healing, the bigger question is, "Why is the person that abused me experiencing so much goodness in their lives?" From the outward, people may see that God is blessing them, but is that truly the case? At points, you will even begin to question whether any of this is true, whether you truly were mentally or emotionally abused and will then begin to wonder if you were as bad to your abuser as they made you out to be. After all, the Bible tells us that we will reap what we sow. *Was the seed that I sowed into the relationship with my abuser actually bad? If not, then why am I not reaping good in my life? Could it be that God is punishing me?* Or could it be that because you are now seeking freedom and beginning to rediscover your true identity in Christ and therefore what you deserve from every relationship in your life, your enemy, the devil, is sending attack after attack against you? You see, your enemy will only guard what he is afraid of. Perhaps the reason so many things appear to be going smoothly for your abuser while you feel that you are struggling is because your abuser is not a threat to the enemy in their current state, but you are extremely dangerous to him. It does not make the struggle any easier or knowing that your abuser is doing well any easier for you to handle. But it can be freeing, knowing that you are on the right path.

Let's break down this frustration step-by-step to discover where our real feelings get exchanged for false information. We start with the emotion of anger. What causes this anger is discovering that good things appear to be happening in the life of our abuser, meanwhile we are experiencing losses in our own lives. This could range from the abuser receiving a new job, house, relationship, pet, vehicle, or any combination of these things or more. However, remember that the abuser is not content in and of themselves. They are constantly seeking validation from other people and constantly in need of receiving new things to keep up their appearances in order for them to feel happy. It is very sad, knowing that they are discontented despite that everything in their new life appears to be going to plan. The idea of being content with what they have is one that will never cross the mind of the narcissist. They may experience fleeting happiness from the person or object that they have deemed as their most important thing to them at this point in their life, but they are never truly content. Still your anger rages at knowing how you treated them and how they treated you in return, just to be replaced by the next best thing that comes across their path. It consumes your thoughts, and you consider how you could approach them with the truth, boldly forcing them to look truth in the face. You must understand that this is a futile effort because to the narcissist, you will always be the person who was in the wrong. Approaching them with the truth will only cause them to respond with quips that not only do not make sense to your current situation but will attempt to draw anger out of you as a person. The vindictive personality of the abuser does not care how they make you feel. All they want is to fill their void with whatever promises to fill it for that specific moment. Their version of the truth grossly neglects the facts from another person's side and only serves to defend themselves.

After discovering the anger caused by the success of your abuser, it is time to discover why. The truth is that in any other case, you would be happy for the success of another person. You would want to celebrate it and allow them to celebrate and be celebrated for the victories that they've accomplished but not in the case of the abuser. You feel that you've done so much for them, and they have discarded you, like you were nothing. The fact is that they did and were able to, not because you were terrible to them but because they did not invest half of what you did into the relationship. You know how well you treated them, yet they continue to be blessed in their life, while you have stepped back and become the object of scorn among former friends, family members, and even people from church. Once again, the abuser spared no expense in running your name into the ground while simultaneously asking you to protect their name. You begin to feel that perhaps, if everyone that was a friend to you and your abuser believes that you were in fact the abuser in the relationship, then perhaps it is true and perhaps God is in fact judging you. This may seem like sound logic, but remember, anyone and everyone that the abuser could get on their side, they have already reached out to and tainted with their half-truth of the situation. You did not try to reach out and get people on your side, rather you chose to keep silent and absorb the abuse for a prolonged period of time. That is an act of true love. Keep in mind also that the Bible says that "in that way, you will be acting as true children of your Father in heaven. For he gives his sunlight to both the evil and the good, and he sends rain on the just and the unjust alike" (Matthew 5:45).

If this is true, then rest assured that not everything is as good as what others may make it out to be, and oftentimes one of the favorite masks that a narcissist will use is that of social media. Hidden safely behind the screen of their mobile device, the abuser runs no risk of their true selves being exposed, which is exactly how they like it. Do not be deceived into believing that everything in their life is perfect. The fact is that you may feel like everything around you is falling apart, but because you are seeking healing the proper way and are attempting to move on with your life, you can have less than they do and *still* be more content than they are. Remember, the narcissist is continuously trying to dress up the outside in an attempt to make everything appear perfect, but on the inside, they are in shambles. Rather than feeling angry for the good things happening to your abuser, this should lead you to feel sorry for them. Realizing and recognizing that they are living in a house of cards, which is one blow from caving in, should lead you to realize and recognize how very lucky you were to get out of the situation you were in. The constant need for more and lack of contentment with life is not something you ever experienced before, and it is not something you need to live with. Rather, you can live full of joy and contentment, knowing that God is in control, and He will handle your every need. The false information that has been presented to you has caused you to believe that there is something inherently wrong with you. You often gaslight yourself and even begin to believe the lies that have been told to you. There are so many layers of false information that have been piled up on you that you have difficulty distinguishing between fact and fiction. This is natural, particularly in the realm of long-term relationships with narcissists. You had always been in the wrong, so how could you possibly be in the right now? What if the truth is that it was not you in the wrong but that your abuser was all along?

Think back to some of your arguments with your abuser. Was the goal of the argument to help build and strengthen the relationship, or was it to justify acts that hurt you? If the goal of the argument was not to help strengthen the relationship, then the fault lands on the person who was trying to justify their actions against the person. This is often accomplished with angry and aggressive behavior on the part of the abuser in an attempt to silence the victim. Why then are we angry to see our abuser happy?—because we have been hurt by someone we truly believed loved and cared about us. In discovering the truth of who our abusers really are, we realize that we were only used and never loved. This realization would cause anyone to become angry, but what if you began to be thankful that this part of your life is over? What if you began to be grateful that you will never have to deal with mediocre treatment ever again? What if you would allow yourself to see this not as a curse but as a blessing? After all, you now have more time and energy to dedicate toward things that genuinely matter to you. You will come to discover in time that your anger will dissipate, and you will find yourself experiencing true joy and happiness in place of your former anxiety, pressure, and anger.

You will be so glad that you did discover the true nature of your abuser.

Upon discovering why your anger toward your abuser exists, there is a final step toward no longer desiring vengeance or justice. This final step is simply accepting the newfound truth as the real truth. This can be remarkably difficult for victims because it means rejecting all lies that you have heard up until this point. The lies that you were loved, needed, wanted, and desired by your abuser were not the truth. You were simply used because you were the best thing available at the time. However, this is a good thing for you to realize because at some point, you were the best option for your abuser. This means that you do have value; you are attractive; you are desirable as a person. The issue is not with you or your quality as a person but rather the mental state of your abuser. The narcissist is incapable of being content, and therefore they cannot be content in any relationship. Once again, this is not your fault. The sad truth is that your abuser was never going to be content, and therefore, you were always going to be in competition with the next best thing. You personally would never have dreamed of giving attention to another person, but in the case of your abuser, there was always another person on their radar that could have been a better fit. Whether the abuser chose to act on their impulses or not, they certainly were not ever fully yours in their minds. The Bible tells us in John 8:31–32, "So Jesus said to the Jews who had believed him, 'If you abide in my word, you are truly my disciples, and you will know the truth, and the truth will set you free.'"

The truths found here can give you a certain sense of moral and confidence boost because, you see, the narcissistic personality is not capable of looking very far past the outward appearance of another person. Oftentimes, if the narcissist is asked what drew them to you as a person, the answer will be superficial in nature. They will respond more often than not that it was your looks in some way, shape, or form. Remember, the outer appearance is what your abuser spent most of their time attempting to be perfect because they were incapable of introspection and believing that there could have been something that they may need to change. They have attempted to cover up their underlying issues with an attractive exterior. This is why they have a need for new things, new ways of dressing up the outside, and new relationships so very often. They are so consumed with the idea of covering up their flaws because they are unwilling to look down deep and consider that their actions and words may have been good for them but that it may have harmed someone that genuinely cared about them. This being the case, of course the outer appearance would be one of the most important criteria to an abuser when selecting a victim. This is often first on their priority list because they have to be able to show you off to their friends and family. And what better way to show off than to have everyone agree that you are attractive? This also gives the abuser a momentary and fleeting sense of happiness because they have attracted an attractive mate. Your attention becomes intoxicating to them, and it becomes the center of their conversation and their proudest possession, that is until the next best thing comes along. Very quickly and almost at the drop of a hat, your abuser changes how they interact with you. Hours-long phone calls diminish to periodic text messages, they no longer take pictures with you to share on their social media, and whenever you reach out to them, you're now portrayed as needy and annoying, instead of caring and sweet.

You were not the one that changed in the relationship, and it was not your fault for the change. The truth is that your abuser became bored and was ready to move on to the next best thing. These truths are freeing, however, because now, rather than doubting how attractive you are, you can be sure that you are plenty attractive. Rather than doubting your character as a person, you can be sure that you were consistent in your relationship, even when your partner changed. Rather than doubting whether you are a good person, you can be sure that you were more than good to someone who treated you abusively. These characteristics do not make you weak; they make you strong because you were willing to fight for something that you believed to be real. You always told yourself that you were extremely lucky to have found your abuser. You considered them to be the most amazing person that you had ever met, but the truth is that they were lucky to have met you. The way that you treated them and the amount of abuse you were willing to put up with was more than enough reason for them to consider themselves lucky. Remember, the outside of the person was the only thing that was receiving any attention because they were incapable of doing any sort of introspection. The abusive person does not want to look inward because they do not want to reveal the mess that compiles their lives. What you fell in love with was not a person but rather the shell of a severely broken human being.

There is peace and joy on the other side of this mental and emotional abuse that you've encountered, and you can be sure that God is a loving Father. He never intended or desired for you to be treated or feel the way that your abuser treated you and made you feel. It is no wonder that you felt angry after all the investment that you made into the relationship, only to discover that you were being used by your abuser. However, knowing why this feeling of anger exists inside of you and then discovering the truth about the inner workings of your abuser can be most freeing. This is because you recognize the truth about yourself as well. You are a good person. You are attractive. You are capable of finding another person that will love you genuinely. The lies that have covered your mind, leading you to believe that you are not good enough or that you don't deserve better than what you received from your abuser, are slowly beginning to fade away. Rest assured that the more distance and time apart from your abuser, the better off you will become. This is because they cannot counteract the truths that are slowly being birthed within you with lies that they have told themselves and others to make you appear to be less than what you were. God gave us all emotions, and it is okay for us to experience them, but eventually emotions must change. There is nothing wrong with you experiencing anger and a desire for justice, but is that truly what you want? The truth is that, as a victim of mental and emotional abuse, all that you want is peace in your life. You want to feel the joy that you experienced prior to your abuser restored. This cannot take place as long as you hold onto hatred, anger, and a desire for justice. Do not rush your process, but eventually you will discover that there is freedom, peace, and joy in releasing the other person from what you feel they owe you. This, believe it or not, is a way for you to allow God to reclaim control over your life. You will no longer have consuming thoughts about your abuser, and in some cases, you may even feel a draw to pray for the person who has hurt you so badly because you now recognize who they truly are and how much they are hurting themselves and not just you.

CHAPTER 5

Thank God for Neuroplasticity

One of the biggest concerns to the victim of mental and emotional abuse is, when will this ever change?—the constant spinning and doubting yourself and whether or not you were a good person to your abuser. The overwhelmingly good news is, yes, it will change in time. This is more torturous than the relationship itself, and it can be difficult to imagine a world in which you no longer think about your abuser and what went wrong. But the good news is that your mind has only been conditioned to believe what you have put into it. For so long, you have allowed your mind to be filled with lies from your abuser and others around you that you now see yourself only according to the lies. It is a freeing thought to consider that perhaps freedom is drawing closer to you every day because you are now replacing those lies with truth. The truth is that your mind was not always conditioned to view yourself the way that you do now. As a matter of fact, if you can think back to a time prior to your abuser, you will remember thinking only the highest about yourself. You would have considered yourself to be one of the best in your field or fields of expertise, and this was only diminished after meeting your abuser. You no longer viewed yourself in the same way because your abuser led you to believe that you were little more than an expendable asset, only called upon when you were needed, and less than desirable. This was all caused by your abuser's own insecurities and not based upon how you truly viewed yourself. However, after being told time and again how you were viewed by your abuser, either by their actions or their words, eventually you began to believe their lies and allowed yourself to begin to identify with them. Your brain was slowly retrained to believe something about yourself that was not true, and the good news is that your brain can be trained again. There is a process and a scientific fact in the realm of psychology, as well as a biblical principle for this idea of retraining your brain. The Bible states it as being transformed by the renewing of your mind, and we will discuss that later on in this chapter, but the psychologists call this the brains neuroplasticity.

The neuroplasticity of the brain can be described as the brain's capability to change the way that it thinks. The brain is made up primarily of fluid, so it is no wonder that when described, the thought processes are compared to water. They are fluid, constantly moving and changing, much like the waves from the ocean or outbound ripples from where you might throw a rock into a pond. Much like both waves and outbound ripples, the movements, or in other words, the way in which you consider a problem or situation in your life is greatly affected by whatever initiated the movement in your mind. If it is a negative thought, then odds are that your thoughts, feelings, and emotions moving forward are going to follow suit. Let's take an interaction with your abuser for instance. Stop here and consider an argument or time that they made you feel bad during your relationship. Odds are that it was all initiated by an action or word that your abuser used against you. This was the wind that created the wave or the rock that created the outbound ripple in your mind. From that one interaction, your entire mood was changed. Yet your abuser simply continued on with their day, as if nothing had happened, determined that they were in the right and that you were in the wrong. Much like the rock or wind, nothing ever truly changed with them. Meanwhile, your mind has become a playground for terrifyingly oppressive thoughts. You begin to view yourself as this horrible person who has so many issues. But you never viewed yourself this way before meeting your abuser, and you've never seemed to have these types of problems in your life before your abuser either. The truth is that your abuser has simply used the neuroplasticity of your brain against you. The abuser is very cool and calculated with how they will do this because they must know that their words are the ones that matter most to you. For this reason, abusers will always do their best to isolate their victims from people in their lives that love them and will speak truth into their relationship with the abuser.

Isolation is one of the most effective tools that an abuser can use against their victim because the victim will slowly begin to develop themselves around whatever the abuser says to them. This goes so far that an emotionally and mentally abusive person will even cause their victims to compromise in their own personal morals and beliefs. For the victim, this often takes place in the idealization stage, where the abuser begins by making the victim their object of adoration and desire. Once this has taken place, and the victim is ensnared, the abuser will begin to devalue the victim because they know that their words of affirmation and adoration has become addictive to the victim. They now know that the words of others in the victim's life do not hold weight in comparison to that of the abuser. In causing the victim to feel isolated, the abuser has created the ultimate mind trap. Now the victim feels that the only person in their lives that matter is the abuser because, since they are this terrible person that the abuser describes, they are just lucky to have someone around, let alone someone that will love them in spite of all their flaws. But truly, this is not love. Rather, this is grossly sick and twisted manipulation on the part of the abuser. The victim's neuroplasticity has been tainted to be used against them by the abuser. The abuser will then work hard to make sure that the victim remains isolated because the truth must never be found out. As long as they have the victim believing that they are lucky to have found them, then the abuser always has the upper hand, and unfortunately, love is little more than a game to be played by the abuser. Removal of strong and caring friends and more specifically the family of the abused victim is of vital importance to the abuser because the victim cannot gather strength from others if they are constantly surrounded by people who are on the side of the abuser. Ever the manipulator, the abuser will say things to insinuate that they spend too much time with the victim's family and not enough with theirs. This oftentimes is grossly misleading because majority of the time that the abuser spends with the victim is spent surrounded by the abuser's family and friends. The abuser will cause the victim to feel guilty about long-time friendships, especially with members of the opposite sex, even though the abuser is free to go out and interact with old friends of the opposite sex and even develop new friendships with other members of the opposite sex.

The story of the relationship is often one of many double standards all falling in favor of the abuser. It is also true that the abuser will often accuse the victim of doing things that the abuser is actually guilty of, particularly after the relationship has ended. For example, the abuser is often very jealous of the attention of the victim and will not accept the victim giving attention of any sort to members of the opposite sex. They will demand that the victim stop contact with any and all members of the opposite sex, yet they will have no problem still engaging with members of the opposite sex regularly on their end. Yet after the relationship has ended, a very twisted version of the truth will come out, where the victim was the person who did not want them having friends of the opposite sex. Once again, this is an isolation tactic because the abuser is very aware of their clear and obvious neglect of the relationship between them and the victim. Oftentimes, for the victim, some of their greatest strength comes from their friends and family of the opposite sex because there is an awareness that they have about the abuser that cannot be understood by the victim. These relational ties can be damaged and can even be destroyed by the abuser because they must keep the victim isolated at all costs. Without the victim constantly being made to feel that they are completely alone, the power that the abuser has over their victim will slowly begin to diminish. This cannot happen because that would mean that the abuser would have lost control over their victim. The isolation brought on by the abuser will cause the victim's neuroplasticity to believe that they truly are all alone and that they must hold on to their abuser at all costs. But once again, prior to meeting your abuser, you never felt all alone; you never felt unwanted; you never felt it was hard for you to make friends. What happened was you began to view yourself through the broken neuroplasticity that your abuser created within your mind. This was not your doing but rather brought on by manipulation and isolation. While isolation covers a great deal of information, it is not the only tool that your abuser will use to change your neuroplasticity to serve them in breaking you as a person. Another way in which your abuser caused your neuroplasticity to work against you was through manipulating how others saw you.

Manipulation is the name of the game for mental and emotional abusers. Up until this point, we have discussed different ways in which your abuser manipulated you. But now it is time to discover how your abuser used others to negatively affect your neuroplasticity. The manipulation that an abuser will use with others will always be disguised. Oftentimes, this will come in the form of creating lofty opinions of you to others, which you must hold up to. If you do not stand up to these stories, you fear that others may begin to view you differently, so you are constantly paying attention to every little whim or fancy that your abuser may express. You develop a work ethic that is exhausting, and you even begin to neglect self-care, which cannot come as a surprise to you as self-love has long since come and gone. But you do not view your situation in this way; rather you believe that this is the way that love's supposed to be. You allow yourself to be conditioned, for fear of the opinions of others, to believe that love is a matter of constantly sacrificing and giving of yourself in order to achieve your abuser's love, affection, and happiness. This may sound odd to you, but love does not require you to sacrifice everything while the other person in the relationship sacrifices nothing. Some of you may be thinking that is not a true statement, and some of you have already considered Jesus's death on the cross. It is very true that Jesus sacrificed everything on the cross, but does His sacrifice alone bring us back into a relationship with God? I'm sure that you're screaming inside yourself that it was right now. However, allow me to pose this thought to you: If Jesus's sacrifice was the only thing required, then would anyone be able to go to hell? The answer to that question is no. Jesus's love and sacrifice do have the power to cover all our sins, but unless we are willing to sacrifice our sin, pride, fear, doubt, anger, etc. to God, then the sacrifice of Jesus means nothing to us. The power of sacrifice only comes after we are also willing to sacrifice our will to His. Even so, in a relationship, we should be willing to sacrifice our happiness for the sake of the other person, but the willingness to sacrifice should be mutual.

In the case of your abuser, I believe that you will see that their happiness always trumped yours. It was always the first priority rather than putting others before themselves. Because your abuser convinced others that you were all things to them and for them at all times, others have viewed you in a way that insists you be super-human. You feel the need to keep up with the lofty opinions that others have of you and therefore cannot simply be you. This is quite different from the person that an abuser will portray the victim as after the relationship ends though. What was once a fairy tale gets twisted and turned into a nightmare. While it is true that this is exactly what happens in the transition from the idealization to the devaluation stage, what others cannot see is that you were never the abuser. Unfortunately, for many victims of narcissistic people, it is also true that you cannot see the truth either. This is why the gas-lighting and confusion takes place in your mind because the truth is that the breakup truly never had anything to do with you. Rather, it had everything to do with the abuse that you suffered. You never portrayed or even thought of yourself as a victim inside of the rela-tionship. But without fail, looking back, you can see time and again how the standard for your abuser was to play the victim. Upon sep-arating from your abuser, it may surprise you to have some of the friends you once had inform you that even during the relationship, your abuser was still attempting to play the victim card, pointing out every tiny flaw or misstep that you may have made and amplifying them to a wildly outrageous proportion. This is once again the abus-er's sad attempt at playing the victim. No matter what you did, it was never going to be good enough because your abuser did not truly love you. They were not in the relationship to love you; rather they were in it to use you for whatever purpose you may have served at the time. No matter the situation you may have found yourself in, know that no one deserves to be treated in this way. The abuser will spare no expense in trying to destroy you after you two have separated, using jagged and cutting words to try to harm you and attack you as a person, even though they have supposedly moved on with their lives. This again causes others to be manipulated into seeing you as a terrible person. It does not matter how hard you may have tried to save the relationship; all that other people will be told is the negative side of who you are. The abuser will use any and all ammunition and even dig into your past to discover new information to use against you.

This is not normal behavior. You, of course, were the person that was left, not your abuser, yet your abuser insists on pinning sole blame on you. The friends you once believed you had have all deserted you and run to the side of your abuser. Once again, the thrashing that you have received from your abuser goes far beyond what you could ever have imagined. How could someone that claimed to love you so deeply aim to harm you so viciously? The truth is that they are suffering far beyond you could ever imagine. The only way that they are able to maintain some sort of sanity is in seeing other people around them suffer. How grossly sick and twisted this is, especially for those that claim the name of Christian. They claim to be followers of Jesus, yet their fruit shows something much different from the love of Jesus. For another human being to be so disgusted and repulsed by themselves that they would be willing to try to destroy another person is beyond sick. It is beyond pitiful. It is revolting. Remember, this is nothing new from the abuser. When you were together, rest assured that they had more than enough negatives to pin on you, despite how well you may have treated them. You were consistently building them up, but it would never be enough because of the lack of self-love and inability to perform any level of introspection. Additionally, you will remember how they used to judge and mistreat others so long as it served their purpose. The way that they maintain themselves has not changed, only the target of their disgraceful behavior. There may be people in your sphere of influence who know you well enough to recognize that your character is not lining up with the half-truths that your abuser has told them. If this is the case, thank God for those friends because they are true and will be strong people for you to turn to in rough times. Hold tight to them, for they know the truth, and you need it spoken to you often. Because of what others have said about you for such a long time, it will take some time for you to truly believe what was true. We must seek truth in what we believe about ourselves, in what others say about us, but there is one last area that you will need to find the truth in. That area is in what God has to say about us.

Have you ever sat and thought, *What does God have to say about me?* The fact is that God has much to say about us and His love for us in His word. So what does God think about us? Well, the truth is that God loves you unconditionally. No matter who you are, where you have gone, or what you have done, God loves you. The love of God cannot be manipulated or bought by cunning words or actions that we might attempt to bring about. It all has to do with the idea of being in a relationship with Him. He wants *you* so desperately that you cannot begin to imagine the love that He has for you. Most of us have bought into the philosophy of whatever happens is meant to be. However, what if this is a broken thought process? This philosophy emphasizes the sovereignty of God or, in other words, His power rather than His goodness. But if we are to believe that there is a reason that everything happens, then where does free will fit in? You prayed so hard and desperately that God would bring you and your abuser back together. You believed that God truly wanted you two together. Well, what if you were right? What if God truly did want that relationship to work out between you and your abuser, but your abuser is determined to go their own way? God will not force His will on anyone; therefore, your abuser has every right to make whatever decision they wish.

Let's look at this from a different perspective though because with the previously mentioned thought process of God's power being greater than His goodness, there appears to be a conflict between God's sovereignty and free will. But what if God's goodness, His faithfulness to His word, and promise of free will trump His sovereignty? God may have had the best in store for you; He may have even told you His plan for your life. But because He is good, He will not force His will on anyone. You may be wondering how this can be. If God did not ever intend for me to be treated the way that I have been by my abuser, then how could it be that He would intend for me to be in an abusive relationship? Perhaps, God intended to use you to change the heart and mind of your abuser. When we have experienced the love of God, we can't help but want to share that love with others around us. You may not have felt that way in a long time, but whether you realize it or not, you were showing your abuser the love of Father God, allowing your own feelings to cave way to the love of God. God's love is not reliant upon the love of another. The only difference is that you are not God. This being the case, your love is dependent upon something. That thing on which you depend is the love of Father God. As time went on in your relationship, you spent gradually more and more time, trying to earn the love and create the happiness of another person. This was never what you were created for. After all, we are known as human beings, not human doings. Simply being ourselves should be more than enough for anyone to love us, just the way that God does. Understanding that God loves and cares about us exactly the way that we are is freeing, and it shows us how we are to love others. In some cases, past trauma can lead a person to become mentally or emotionally abusive. Trauma can be overcome with God's love, but God will not force His love on anyone. Your abuser may not choose the love that you offer, but this is no reflection on you. Rejection of your love is merely your abuser not understanding the love of a Heavenly Father. This confusion can come to us as well; this is why we can experience anger and confusion at points in the healing journey. But rest assured that you showing your abuser unconditional love was no sign of weakness. Rather it was a sign of strength and knowing who you truly are in Christ.

To wrap up this chapter, remember that God designed your brain in such a way that it can be retrained. The areas you must retrain your brain is in how you view yourself, who you choose to surround yourself with, and finally rediscovering how God sees you. It can help us to understand how God sees us when we see how we loved our abuser, but we must constantly return to the source of our unconditional love. While it is true that the love of God may never run out, ours is capable of doing so if we do not return to the source to refill it. The only place we can go to experience the love of Father God is in His loving presence because going to another person for love will never work. A person's love cannot be fully complete because they are not God. However, rather than jumping into a new relationship or attempting to rebuild an old one, now is the time for you to receive healing and redevelop your love relationship with Jesus. Return to the source, and allow yourself to be truly loved, just for who you are. This is where the first part of this book ends and the second part of the book begins. Understanding the facts and what led up to where you are now is important because it gives us clarity and wisdom of what has transpired, but just as important is discovering where to go and how to respond to the trauma of mental and emotional abuse. The love of God is stronger than any pain or fear that you may have experienced, and He specializes in healing. Now that you have an understanding of the truth, it is time for us to begin the journey of complete restoration.

PART 2

Restoration

Thus far, it should come as no surprise to you that all we have been doing is discussing the facts of mental and emotional abuse. As stated earlier in this book, not many people are aware of or even think about emotional and mental abuse, particularly in the church world, unless they have been affected by it in a very direct way. For this reason, there are many Christian people and even pastors who will live their entire lives in a state of abuse without even realizing it. As it is, when a person is living in this state, they will not notice it because the abuser is cunning and will disguise their abuse in a plethora of ways and then cover it up through gaslighting their victim. The purpose of the first part of the book, therefore, was to give us an understanding of what mental and emotional abuse is. But now, it's time for us to redirect our focus on where it truly belongs. While it is true that you were sickly abused by someone who claimed to love you, the good news is that you are still here, and because of that, God still has good plans for your life.

> "For I know the plans I have for you,"
> declares the Lord, "plans to prosper you and
> not to harm you, plans to give you hope and a
> future." (Jeremiah 29:11)

So far, the journey has been painful for you, much like tearing open an old wound. Reliving the pain that you experienced is not a place any one of us wants to be, but I assure you that having this newfound understanding of your former significant other will help in the healing process, for you will come to find that you deserved and do still deserve so much better. Please note that this is not intended to be a license to leave your abuser. Only you can determine where God is leading and guiding you, but know that God is a loving Father and that He only gives good gifts to His children.

> Every good and perfect gift is from above, coming down from the Father of the heavenly lights, who does not change like shifting shadows. (James 1:17)

I would also encourage you to speak with a Christian brother or sister that has been through divorce before considering the idea. The truth is that divorce hurts, especially when separating from a narcissist; things become much uglier than you could imagine. However, back to the task at hand, the next part of this book will help us to begin the healing process of dealing with mental and emotional abuse and allow us to claim our lives back so that we can truly begin to live again. If you're ready to drop your anger and need for vengeance, then continue on and get ready to live the vibrant life that God has always planned for you.

CHAPTER 6

Your Need for Father's Love

Looking back, you have now discovered that you have not been yourself for a very long time. You feel like you have become little more than a shell of a person and are unsure of who you really are. For this reason, you have come to the place of gaslighting yourself and considering that you may very well be mentally ill and that there may be something wrong with you. The fact is that if you are even considering that there might be something wrong with you or that you might have done something wrong, then all this is gaslighting. The good news is that, eventually, this thought pattern will be broken. Eventually, the truth will be discovered because as you take inventory of the past, you will begin to see the truth. This is why it is so important for you to know who you are in the eyes of God. It is so easy to be deceived because you truly did love your abuser. We must be careful because the heart can convince us into doing some rather crazy things.

> The heart is deceitful above all things and beyond cure. Who can understand it? (Jeremiah 17:9)

This chapter will discuss our need for Father God's love. It is important that we experience His love because we have not experienced true love in so very long, and we were made for a relationship with Him.

Entirely too many people receive poor counseling in the realm of marriages from well-meaning pastors because of lack of information on the subject of mental and emotional abuse. It is sad to think that a person would be told that they are terrible for wanting to leave an abusive spouse. The truth is that in a physically abusive relationship, most pastors encourage their congregants to leave the abusive spouse for the victim's own safety. However, when it comes to mental or emotional abuse, pastors simply tell the victims that they are terrible for considering leaving or that they need to pray for God to change the heart of their abuser or, worse yet, that God would change the heart of the victim. This alone could drive a person to insanity or suicide as they are led to believe that they are a terrible person for wanting to get free from a mental and emotional abuser. In cases like this, there must always be life over law. The value of a human being's life should be worth more than the laws that have been established. After all, is that not what Jesus did?

> One Sabbath Jesus was going through the grainfields, and his disciples began to pick some heads of grain, rub them in their hands and eat the kernels. Some of the Pharisees asked, "Why are you doing what is unlawful on the Sabbath?" Jesus answered them, "Have you never read what David did when he and his companions were hungry? He entered the house of God, and taking the consecrated bread, he ate what is lawful only for priests to eat. And he also gave some to his companions." Then Jesus said to them, "The Son of Man is Lord of the Sabbath." (Luke 6:1–5)

We see here clearly that Jesus has broken a Jewish law. However, the purpose is not to create anarchy but rather to show that He values the quality of a man's life over the law that He Himself had established! God's love for people surpasses the laws that He established for us as guidelines to help us walk in our relationship with Him. For a lot of Christian leaders, that's going to be hard to swallow, but the truth is there. Not only did Jesus do work on the Sabbath by healing a man, but then he permitted His disciples to thresh wheat so that they had something to eat. Even so, in situations of mental and emotional abuse, we should be open to hearing what is truly happening in a relationship before casting judgment. It may very well be that God is trying to improve the quality of a person's life, but because we are so strictly following the law, we miss what Jesus is doing right in front of us.

The love of the Father goes beyond just this idea of life over law because it also shows us who we are to Him. Until you recognize who you really are in Christ, you cannot break free of the lies that you have been told about yourself. As we've learned, your abuser was a master manipulator and therefore has planted all sorts of wrong and deceitful thoughts in your mind concerning who you really are. It is sick and deplorable that a person who claims to love you would lead you to believe that you must earn their love or that you were anything but fully loved by them. This creates a broken thought process, where the victim believes that they are not good enough and therefore need to earn the love of everyone in their lives, including the love of Father God. Rather than knowing that they are unconditionally loved simply for who they are, victims develop the mindset and belief that they are always lacking and in need of improvement in order to earn the love of others. God tells us quite the opposite, however, as He informs us that we could never do anything to lessen His love or earn more of His love. This is what we know as unconditional love and is often the hang-up for a victim in a mentally and emotionally abusive relationship. You see, someone is not capable of giving what they have not received. Therefore, a Christian who has received the full and unconditional love of Jesus will attempt to pour that love into their relationship with their abuser, and well they should, for the Bible says, "Husbands, love your wives, just as Christ loved the church and gave himself up for her" (Ephesians 5:25).

However, a narcissistic person may well not have received this type of love because if they had received this level of love, they would pour out in kind. Jesus Himself gives us directives on how to discover whether a person has been the recipient of true unconditional love when He tells us that "You will know them by their fruits. Do men gather grapes from thornbushes or figs from thistles? Even so, every good tree bears good fruit, but a bad tree bears bad fruit. A good tree cannot bear bad fruit, nor can a bad tree bear good fruit. Every tree that does not bear good fruit is cut down and thrown into the fire. Therefore by their fruits you will know them" (Matthew 7:15–20).

This is a standard case of actions speaking louder than words, and unfortunately, entirely too many people are fooled by the words of a mental and emotional abuser. However, the emphasis here is not what you did not receive from your abuser but rather what you should be receiving from Father God. It is imperative that you begin to see yourself once again as valuable and, beyond that, that you are worthy of love, not because of what you have done or are capable of but because of what Jesus has done for you and what He is capable of through you! The moment that you accepted Jesus's forgiveness through His blood on the cross, your past was washed away, and He no longer viewed you as a sinful creature but rather as a righteous son or daughter of Christ. Whether you realize it or not, this makes you significant.

Choosing to recognize yourself as significant means putting yourself back out there and being willing to take chances on what you feel God is calling you to do. To be honest, writing this book has been a huge test of my faith, but I knew that I had to do something different and that I needed to get back out and take some chances on myself. This is no easy task for the person who has been in a mentally or emotionally abusive relationship though because, oftentimes, the person has been belittled and devalued to a place where there self-confidence has been shattered. Odds are, before you entered into the relationship with your abuser, you were a confident person and truly believed in yourself and your own capabilities. However, as you began to open up and share your dreams with your abuser, you slowly allowed each one to fall by the wayside. This was not because you truly didn't believe in yourself but rather because, time and again, your goals and dreams were met with condescension and hurtful words that led you to believe that you were incompetent to make them into realities. There are a few things you must understand about this behavior though. First, it is not based on the person's love for you. If you truly felt like you wanted to do something and that you were capable of doing it, then your significant other should have backed and supported you however they could have. It is normal for a person to want to see their significant other succeed. Even so, it is standard that God wants to see us succeed. His desire has always been to see us participate alongside Him in making His call on our lives become a reality. Rest assured that if you have a God-sized dream, that has to do with building God's kingdom, that He will provide what you need to fulfill that call on your life. You are significant, and the call that God has placed on your life matters! The Bible tells us that "indeed, the very hairs of your head are all numbered. Don't be afraid; you are worth more than many sparrows" (Luke 12:7).

If God cares about you enough to know the number of hairs on your head, then you can be sure that His call on your life is far more significant than you can ever begin to imagine. You have significance, and you matter to God. At the end of the day, this is much more significant than being admired or cared about by other people. If God views you as this significant, then rest assured that you are. It is a matter of relearning who you are at this point and reminding yourself daily that you have value. Just because you were devalued by one person in your life does not mean that you have no value. It is true that your abuser may have dragged other people onto their side by saying all sorts of terrible things about you to them, but then, was that really love? And if those people that were in both you and your abuser's life truly cared about you, then why did they not come to you when your abuser began to spill out all of these hateful and hurtful things about you? Odds are, those friends were not truly for you as a person, and odds are still further that you were never valuable to them either. Unfortunately, due to a lack of knowledge on this subject, many churchgoers and even pastors will find themselves in the exact same boat, going to comfort the poor narcissistic person while the victim is left on their own to attempt to pick up the pieces. Even more unfortunately, the victim, by this time, has most likely lost sight of themselves and forgotten who they truly are and will begin to act inconsistently with who they really are. They may begin to act out and seek refuge from unhealthy coping mechanisms, such as drugs, alcohol, or sex. This does not nullify the victim's responsibility for their actions; however, there is always cause and effect in relationship. And rather than taking ownership for their part in driving the victim to this point, the abuser is perfectly content to use the poor coping skills that the victim is using as more ammunition to destroy the victim's reputation. Friendships were never intended to operate in this way. As a matter of fact, they were intended to do the exact opposite of what is described here! The Bible tells us in Proverbs, "As iron sharpens iron, so one person sharpens another" (Proverbs 27:17).

At this point, it would be an injustice for me to overlook that a person cannot consistently act in a way that is inconsistent with who they really are. The person who is acting out of pain will eventually come back to themselves and redevelop their relationship with God. However, in seeking restoration, which Jesus calls us to, there will be people inside of the church, even pastors, that will dismiss their return to Christ as fake and choose to continue backing the abusive party. This is the level to which, in the world of psychology, the narcissist will groom their flying monkeys. Instead of choosing to love the returning person into a deeper relationship with Jesus, those that have been groomed by the narcissist will dismiss the attempts of reconciliation by the victim and ultimately dismiss the true victim while backing and supporting the abuser. This feels unfair and hurtful for the victim, but in the end, it is best that they choose to remember that they have value and to go and seek a new circle of friendship, where they will be backed and supported as they should have been in the first place.

When you think back on your life, however, I'm sure that this sense of being devalued was the exception and not the norm. We, as human beings, were built to be in relationship with each other, for we were made in the image of God according to Genesis 1:27.

> So God created mankind in his own image,
> in the image of God he created them; male and
> female he created them.

This does not speak merely to the physical buildup of human beings but our mental and relational capacity as well. God has always been in relationship. Whether that was with Adam and Eve, the angels, or Himself, God has always been in relationship. And because of this, we too can understand that we were built for relationships. This is why we must be careful what type of relationships we allow ourselves into. For most churchgoers, I am sure that mental and emotional abuse was not something that you regularly heard about from the pulpit. Because of lack of knowledge, we are then open and susceptible to mentally and emotionally abusive relationships. This is not because we are bad people or that we deserve to be hurt in the ways that we have been but because of lack of knowledge and understanding that there are narcissistic people out there, and we should be aware of what they are capable of. Every relationship that you have should be encouraging you and causing you to grow stronger, not just as a person but in your relationship with God as well.

Because you have experienced devaluation for so long however, you are most likely going to begin gaslighting yourself, and your abuser will make sure that happens by empowering their flying monkeys with all the ammunition they can handle. This is why it is so important for you to first and foremost rediscover your identity in Christ. Knowing the truth about what has happened to you through the course of your relationship with the narcissist can be very difficult because the narcissist will stop at nothing to make sure they keep you off-balance. The best way to do that is by keeping you guessing and confused. However, when the truth is revealed, and it bursts forth in your spirit, it is then that you can experience true freedom. We read in John 8, "So Jesus said to the Jews who had believed him, 'If you abide in my word, you are truly my disciples, and you will know the truth, and the truth will set you free'" (John 8:31–32).

There is a big difference between head knowledge and heart knowledge. Simply being made aware of facts is not enough because the narcissist, at any given point, is capable of twisting and changing the truth, and they will, at all costs, maintain their victim mentality. It is therefore crucial for survivors to develop fundamental truths about who they are. Who does God say that you are? Is that consistent with what the narcissist has shown you? If not, one of them is a liar, and I'll give you a hint: It is not God. With this in mind, you must ask yourself whether having this person in your life is going to help you fulfill God's call on your life or not. If not, then perhaps it is time for you to break ties. This can be especially difficult for a Christian going through a divorce with children involved. However, rest assured that it is always best for your children to see the truth, even if it hurts. You choosing to see who you really are in Christ. And choosing to love yourself enough to establish boundaries is a healthy practice for a person to be in. Remember, a person cannot love others if they are incapable of loving themselves. Eventually, facing the fact that remaining depressed and frustrated does not benefit either you or your children is a crucial step in recovering the real you. Perhaps you were holding out hope that someday your relationship with the narcissist would be rebuilt. However, would that actually be beneficial? Is that actually God's best for you? Understanding that God is a loving Father, Who only wants the best for you, can be incredibly freeing! Perhaps your miracle did not come in the form of a restored relationship but rather in the form of *your* restoration. You being restored to the person you were before the narcissistic abuse and being devalued is much better than returning to the brokenness of a narcissistic relationship. You are free to be yourself again! You can enjoy the things that you value and enjoy! Come to find out, it is okay for you to enjoy your life! It may seem like you have given up your faith in a restored relationship, but what if your hope has not been taken, just directed toward something that is more meaningful? What if seeing yourself the way that God sees you is more important to God than following a stringent list of rules and guidelines? For some of you, this may seem like anarchy or as though we are deviating from the truth. However, did Jesus not do this exact same thing? We read in Luke 6:1–5, "One Sabbath Jesus was going through the grainfields, and his disciples began to pick some heads of grain, rub them in their hands and eat the kernels. Some of the Pharisees asked, 'Why are you doing what is unlawful on the Sabbath?' Jesus answered them, 'Have you never read what David did when he and his companions were hungry? He entered the house of God, and taking the consecrated bread, he ate what is lawful only for priests to eat. And he also gave some to his companions.' Then Jesus said to them, The Son of Man is Lord of the Sabbath.'"

You see, Jesus was more concerned about the well-being of the man with the withered hand and His disciples than following a list of stringent guidelines. What if God has something better planned for you? It may seem that you are in a season of suffering right now. However, what if God has allowed for certain things to happen and take place because He has something better planned? Remember that the Bible tells us in Jeremiah 29:11, "'For I know the plans I have for you,' declares the Lord, 'plans to prosper you and not to harm you, plans to give you hope and a future.'"

All the questions, anger, frustrations, and confusion you are feeling is very normal. Do not feel like you are the only person that has ever encountered this type of abuse. You are not alone. However, remember that to a narcissist, everything is about maintaining control. Their very lives are a constant state of manipulation and lying because they do not love themselves. Down deep, the narcissist struggles with being able to look themselves in the mirror and just be honest about who they are. This is why they are consistently and constantly looking for new ways to dress up their outside and make themselves appear to be better off than what they truly are. This is also why a narcissist will rush into a new relationship after yours has ended. It has nothing to do with your value or what you brought to the table in your relationship. Because the narcissist needs a consistent supply of affirmation, they will learn to move on quickly so as to not ever be in lack of a source of supply. You were not a human being to your narcissist but rather a source of affirmation. But again, this lie that you were not enough or good enough simply is not true. Jesus, after all, was willing to give His very life for you. Even if it was only you, He would still have done this for you.

❧

CHAPTER 7

Rumination, Grief, and Newfound Freedom

You now know that it is for the best that you have separated from your narcissist, so why do you still feel this sickening, dark feeling inside of you? Oftentimes, victims of mental and emotional abuse will view this as them wondering if they were the one that made a mistake. However, this simply is not true. There is so much hidden beneath the surface that needs to be unpackaged. It all starts with being willing to step into the dark thoughts that seem to overwhelm you. This is no easy task because your mind has already been overwhelmed by your abuser through gaslighting, future faking, manipulation, and lying. Being sure that you are mentally armed with the truths, you need to combat the lies that have been told to you about yourself. It is the first step in this process. This may take time for you to get to; however, it is fundamental to your healing. Recognizing that what happened to you was not okay and that you did and do deserve better is a necessary piece to your healing process. In this chapter, we will be looking at a moment in the life of Jesus that required rumination, grieving, and living with no regrets. The Bible says in John 11:1–44, "Now a man named Lazarus was sick. He was from Bethany, the village of Mary and her sister Martha. (This Mary, whose brother Lazarus now lay sick, was the same one who poured perfume on the Lord and wiped his feet with her hair.) So the sisters sent word to Jesus, 'Lord, the one you love is sick.' When he heard this, Jesus said, 'This sickness will not end in death. No, it is for God's glory so that God's Son may be glorified through it.' Now Jesus loved Martha and her sister and Lazarus. So when he heard that Lazarus was sick, he stayed where he was two more days, and then he said to his disciples, 'Let us go back to Judea. 'But Rabbi,' they said, 'a short while ago the Jews there tried to stone you, and yet you are going back?' Jesus answered, 'Are there not twelve hours of daylight? Anyone who walks in the daytime will not stumble, for they see by this world's light. It is when a person walks at night that they stumble, for they have no light.' After he had said this, he went on to tell them, 'Our friend Lazarus has fallen asleep; but I am going there to wake him up.' His disciples replied, 'Lord, if he sleeps, he will get better.' Jesus had been speaking of his death, but his disciples thought he meant natural sleep. So then he told them plainly, 'Lazarus is dead, and for your sake I am glad I was not there, so that you may believe. But let us go to him.' Then Thomas (also known as Didymus) said to the rest of the disciples, 'Let us also go, that we may die with him.' On his arrival, Jesus found that Lazarus had already been in the tomb for four days. Now Bethany was less than two miles from Jerusalem, and many Jews had come to Martha and Mary to comfort them in the loss of their brother. When Martha heard that Jesus was coming, she went out to meet him, but Mary stayed at home. 'Lord,' Martha said to Jesus, 'if you had been here, my brother would not have died. But I know that even now God will give you whatever you ask.' Jesus said to her, 'Your brother will rise again.' Martha answered, 'I know he will rise again in the resurrection at the last day.' Jesus said to her, 'I am the resurrection and the life. The one who believes in me will live, even though they die; and whoever lives by believing in me will never die. Do you believe this?' 'Yes, Lord,' she replied, 'I believe that you are the Messiah, the Son of God, who is to come into the world.' After she had said this, she went back and called her sister Mary aside. 'The Teacher is here,' she said, 'and is asking for you.' When Mary heard this, she got up quickly and went to him. Now Jesus had not yet entered the village, but was still at the place where Martha had met him. When the Jews who had been with Mary in the house, comforting her, noticed how quickly she got up and went out, they followed her, supposing she was going to the tomb to mourn there.

When Mary reached the place where Jesus was and saw him, she fell at his feet and said, 'Lord, if you had been here, my brother would not have died.' When Jesus saw her weeping, and the Jews who had come along with her also weeping, he was deeply moved in spirit and troubled. 'Where have you laid him?' he asked. 'Come and see, Lord,' they replied. Jesus wept. Then the Jews said, 'See how he loved him!' But some of them said, 'Could not he who opened the eyes of the blind man have kept this man from dying?' Jesus, once more deeply moved, came to the tomb. It was a cave with a stone laid across the entrance. 'Take away the stone,' he said. 'But, Lord,' said Martha, the sister of the dead man, 'by this time there is a bad odor, for he has been there four days.' Then Jesus said, 'Did I not tell you that if you believe, you will see the glory of God?' So they took away the stone. Then Jesus looked up and said, 'Father, I thank you that you have heard me. I knew that you always hear me, but I said this for the benefit of the people standing here, that they may believe that you sent me.' When he had said this, Jesus called in a loud voice, 'Lazarus, come out!' The dead man came out, his hands and feet wrapped with strips of linen, and a cloth around his face. Jesus said to them, 'Take off the grave clothes and let him go.'"

It is actually foundational to beginning the healing process for this next chapter because no matter who you are, since you have lived in devaluation for so long, you will ruminate into your past relationship. You will try to figure out what you did wrong and discover how you should change. You will ruminate on the good times and wish for those back. However, whatever you choose to ruminate on, the universal truth is that you *will* ruminate. Once you have taken control of your mind and chosen to not allow your mind to spin through rumination, you will begin to grieve. This is natural for a person to grieve when they have lost something. For this reason, it is important for the survivor to recognize what they are actually grieving. What you are grieving is not the loss of the person in the relationship. For some, it is grieving the loss of potentially breaking the generational curse of divorce, grieving raising your children in a home where both parents are present, grieving the loss of your innocence, grieving the loss of a life that was promised to you by your narcissist. There is a lot to grieve, and it is not one dimensional. Allowing yourself to grieve is a natural process after having lost something. This eventually leads into the final step for this chapter, and that is recognizing that you have no regrets. But we will get more into that later. For now, let's take a look at this first step of rumination.

Rumination is more than just remembering the past. It is a state of victimhood where the survivor has yet to reclaim their mental processes. Rather than you controlling your mind, your mind continues to control you. The end result is that the survivor finds themselves in a never-ending cycle of negative thought processes in which they feel that they have somehow done wrong or harmed the other person. Once again, due to gaslighting, devaluation, and belittling of their feelings by the abuser, the victim is stuck in a vortex of thoughts that constantly drown out the best experiences in life. In many cases, the survivor will actually begin to think that they have gone crazy not being able to believe what they know to be true and choosing instead to believe that this abuser could not be this heartless being that is described here. When the truth is cast to the wayside, all that remains is confusion and lack of understanding of what just happened to the victim. In many cases, this results in large releases of pent-up frustration in anger. It is actually very sad to see a person walking through this process because they cannot see a way out of their pain. It does not matter how many people have told them that they are better off without their abuser. The victim will live in this for a season, especially if the narcissist has already moved on, and we know that they will move on sooner than the victim, seeing the love bombing stage take place with another victim causes pain to the victim but rest assured that a person cannot consistently act in a way that is inconsistent with their character. The narcissist does not change because there is never a reason to change. Therefore, what you are witnessing is merely a facade, and rest assured that the poor treatment you received while under your narcissist's spell is also coming for the new source of narcissistic supply. In the same way, I am sure that Jesus ruminated on the life of His friend Lazarus. After all, this was in the first century when this all took place, and therefore, there were no planes, trains, or vehicles that could make travel more quickly. As a matter of fact, most travel was done on foot. Now, I don't know about you, but if I'm Jesus, I'm in a hurry to get to my friend Lazarus's house and help Him. You can almost imagine Jesus beginning to think about all the good times that he and Lazarus had as He began to make His way through the city. Jesus knew what was about to happen; however. he chose to remain in the city and do ministry. It was not until after Lazarus had died that Jesus began the journey toward Lazarus's house. Can you imagine the memories they must have had together? The Bible says that Lazarus was one of Jesus's very best friends. So can you imagine being the best friend of Jesus as a teenager? Not only was Jesus one of Lazarus best friends, but He also was aware of who He was, so He knew that one day soon, He would be dying for His friend. In this case, the rumination that Jesus was experiencing must have been overwhelming.

Jesus's relationship with Lazarus and the loss of your narcissist have something in common. There is a trigger, which sends us into rumination. That trigger of course is loss. Loss is not the best feeling in the world, but rumination often hides what has truly been lost behind the guise of remembering only the good. It is few and far between that someone will bring up negative memories of a deceased person at their funeral. This is because the sense of loss leads us to feel that whatever we lost must have been something good. However, if we can turn down the rumination and feeling of loss, we receive an eagle's eye view of what we really lost. Taking time to step back and grab our bearings is what most people that have been in a mentally and emotionally abusive relationship need the most. This is because the narcissist loves to maintain control over their victims and the best way they know how to do that is by making sure that they are off-balance. The best way that a narcissist can do this is through confusion, which often comes in the form of gaslighting or future faking. In the case of Jesus, He was aware that He had lost someone that was a true friend, and the stroll down memory lane could not have been an easy one for Him. Can you imagine the conversation that Jesus might have had with Father God? But in the case of your narcissist, it is imperative that you recognize what you truly lost and not just what the narcissist wishes you to see. Again, seeing the love bombing from your narcissist being flung onto another person can be paralyzing. For this reason, it is best that separation takes place. The reason why is because what is being portrayed is a false representation of the person that you had been in a relationship with. After separation, you can begin to see the true nature of your relationship with the narcissist. And as you are not seeing all of the love bombing first hand, you are allowed a clear picture of the person that you had been in a relationship with. The reality is that a vast majority of your relationship was not real. Now everything did actually take place that you remember. But as you begin to look back, even on the good times, you can clearly see how miserable you were and how your narcissist had slowly sucked your very humanity out of you. This may seem like a pretty drastic statement, but it is true. Being in a narcissistic relationship is more dehumanizing than you can imagine because the narcissist devalues you, and eventually, you begin to see yourself in the very light that they want to shine on you. Once you are fully aware of the truth and how mistreated you truly were inside of this mentally and emotionally abusive relationship, you will begin to reduce the amount of time that you spend ruminating. You will no longer have this person circling in your mind on a 24-7 basis, and that is a very large step in your healing process. Rumination has the power to leave us paralyzed and defenseless against any attacks that the narcissist may wage. And please be aware that narcissists are crafty, cold, and calculated. This simply means that they are very strategic with how they will interact with you, and they want to know that you are not okay. Almost as intoxicating as the love bombing stage is the discarding stage for the narcissist, for they wish to see the person who once had so much going for them destroyed, this feeds the narcissist's ego and leads them to believe that they have gotten away with all of their mistreatment of you. Now that you see your abuser for who they really are, it is time to move forward in the process of healing and go from rumination to grief.

Grief is a very natural part of the human cycle of loss. Even Jesus experienced grief when He lost His friend Lazarus. We read, after all, that "Jesus wept." The feelings associated with loss can be very difficult for survivors to understand. The difficulty that most survivors of narcissistic abuse face about grief is, they often confuse it with remorse or conviction. In most cases, once grief sets in, it leads the survivor to believe that they must have done something wrong and, therefore, begin to grieve the loss of their narcissistic partner, once again taking all of the blame on themselves. Living in this state is exactly where the narcissist wants you, and it is not a good state for anyone to be in. Taking responsibility for another person's actions while the abuser remains blameless is completely broken and twisted, especially when another human being is doing this to a person they claim to have loved. This also creates doubt in the mind of the survivor as to whether they were actually in the wrong in the relationship. This is broken thinking brought on by gaslighting, love bombing, and future faking by the narcissist. Feeling remorse whatsoever is not something that a narcissist is capable of, so as a survivor the fact that you are feeling remorse over things that were not your fault in the relationship is a clear sign that you are not the narcissist. Breaking this thought pattern takes time, and it usually helps to solidify truth if you got no contact with the narcissist. The sickening sense that you have in your spirit is one that your narcissist placed inside of you. Telling you that you were not good enough for them still screams loudly in your spirit and causes you to believe that if you were not good enough for them, then you will never be good enough for anyone else. Survivor, *this…is…a…lie.* You need not grieve the loss of a person that did not value you the way you deserved to be valued. Yet down deep, you still have a sickening feeling, as if there is something wrong. As stated before, it is universal that you will experience grief when going through loss in your life. However, understanding that everything your relationship with your narcissist was based on a lie gives us clarity as to what we are actually grieving. You should not be grieving the loss of your narcissist now that you see and know their true colors. So if you are not grieving the person, then what are you actually grieving? The answer is complex because the nature of your relationship with your narcissist was also complex. You may be grieving several things at once, which may include getting a divorce when you swore you never would, breaking up a home for your children, hope that things would get better if you held on just a little bit longer, universally you will grieve the loss of friends and people that were in both you and your narcissist's inner circle, and there is plenty more that you may be grieving. Unfortunately, that is up to you to unpack, as grieving is very personal in nature because it deals with something that you have personally lost. Knowing the things you are grieving, however, can help you come to terms and heal more quickly because you no longer are ruminating on the individual; you now can accept the losses that you experienced and continue in your healing journey. Jesus recognized the loss of His friend, and He was able to work through it in a healthy way. As a survivor, the loss of your relationship with the narcissist should be able to work the same way. Even so, we now must recognize what we truly lost. In grieving what was actually lost, a survivor can begin to heal and begin to walk in a normal head state again, perhaps for the first time since meeting their narcissist.

After you have taken the step to stop ruminating, and you have grieved the things which were actually lost in the relationship, it is now time to choose to live without your narcissist. This step, in the title, is called newfound freedom, and you will find that is exactly what this final step in this chapter is about because you begin to realize that the narcissist will not change their ways. They have been so accustomed to using and abusing people throughout their lives that they see no reason to change things now. Why would they? They continually get away with idealizing, devaluing, and finally discarding their victims with no consequences to their actions, so why would your situation be any different? Without any real consequences to their actions, there is no reason for the narcissist to make changes in their patterns that have always worked for them. For this reason, a survivor must ask themselves why they would ever return to such a harmful relationship. The hope found inside the heart of the believing survivor is that, one day, the narcissistic person will change and become the person that they always claimed to be. For this reason, seeing the narcissistic person in their newfound relationship is very difficult for the survivor and can even cause the survivor to believe that the reason for the breakdown in the relationship was solely their fault. This, however, is a lie. What you are witnessing is the love bombing stage, which the narcissist continually uses to draw in their victims until they become bored and determined that the victim is no longer worthy of their time or attention. Do not be deceived into believing that the narcissist is either capable of or willing to change because there is no desire to change inside of the heart of a narcissist. There is only one way that a narcissist will truly change the way that they engage with others, and that is if they have a dynamic encounter with Jesus. Returning to the story of Lazarus, it is interesting to see that Lazarus remained in the tomb and that nothing at all changed for him until Jesus showed up. Once Jesus was there, He was able to call Lazarus out of the darkness of the tomb and back to life. Even so, with the life of a narcissist, until Jesus shows up and calls them out of the way in which they engage with others, it will not be possible for them to change. It is only through the narcissist recognizing who they truly are and then choosing to change, that a victim can truly hope for the restoration of a relationship with their abuser. This fact alone is freeing because the survivor of mental and emotional abuse can truly choose to move on with their lives. Please note that this moving on does not come from a place of anger or bitterness but rather from a place of freedom and joy because the survivor of the narcissistic abuser can now recognize who the narcissist is and that the narcissist has no desire to change who they are. While this may be hard to believe for the survivor, it is the truth, which will allow you to be set free from returning to more narcissistic abuse. The reason why so many people in abusive relationships will return to their abusers is because of the misplaced hope, which they hold in their narcissistic abuser.

To recap on this last chapter, a good next step is for you to stop constantly spinning and reliving parts of the relationship you had with your narcissist. This will take time because you currently cannot imagine your life without them. But you will move on and you will live your life again. The first step is to stop allowing yourself to give your past relationship with your abuser so much bandwidth and energy. It will become more natural as time progresses. However, it is also important for you to grieve the actual losses you are experiencing. This means recognizing what has actually been lost in comparison to what your narcissist wants you to believe that you have lost. Upon doing so, you will begin to recognize that what you lost is not greater than what you have the potential to gain as a result of the loss. This then opens the door for you to begin walking in a newfound freedom. This begins by recognizing who your abuser truly is and choosing to live in the freedom of knowing that they have not truly changed. This then allows for you as a person to begin living your life more fully and recognizing who you truly are in Christ. With this comes the freedom to begin to live in the call that God has given you. But we will discuss that in more detail in chapter 10. The next step to walking out in this newfound freedom is choosing how you will respond; not only to your narcissistic abuser, but other narcissistic persons, which you will undoubtedly encounter in the future. Freedom does not mean that we walk around with a chip on our shoulder the rest of our lives, believing that every person we encounter may be narcissistic or choosing to live in victimhood. This also does not mean that we choose to forgive and forget what the narcissist has done to us. Please understand, while forgiveness is a key step to living in freedom and beginning to live our lives again, forgetting what has happened and choosing to live as a scapegoat or doormat for the narcissist is not. This means, choosing to engage your abuser in a way, where you do not wish bad on them, you do not wish well on them, you simply do not wish on them at all—this is a step of becoming completely indifferent to the narcissistic person, and it is the subject matter of the next chapter.

CHAPTER 8

Not Good, Not Bad, Just Indifferent

A lot of Christians will probably have difficulty with this chapter. That's understandable because as a Christian, I also had difficulty in understanding this concept of not wishing good or bad on a person but simply becoming indifferent to them. One large reason why is because inside of the church world, we have been taught to be more peacekeepers rather than peacemakers. Peacekeepers are individuals that will avoid conflict and simply choose to forgive, no matter the offense, because we believe that all conflict is bad. This is a terrible mistruth that has snuck into our world, because all conflict is not bad. It is an unresolved conflict, which is bad. Unresolved conflict has a tendency to fester and cause issues in relationships, which we have with others. But if we can resolve the conflicts we are having, then we become peacemakers because we bring peace by resolving conflicts, which we have in our relationships with others. Therein lies the issue with trying to restore relationships with narcissistic abusers. Because the narcissist is incapable of recognizing their faults in their relationships with others or empathizing with the pain they have caused to others, conflict will always result in the tearing down and dehumanization of the victim. Therefore, the best thing that a survivor of mental and emotional abuse can do is choose to forgive the narcissist for what they have done to them and then choose to move on with their lives. This breaking of ties can cause more backlash in the beginning, but in this particular case, keeping your own peace and maintaining the truth you have come to understand, know, and believe is worth it. This chapter will help us understand better what this idea of becoming indifferent to our narcissistic abuser looks like from the very words of Jesus. In this particular portion of scripture, Jesus was instructing His disciples in the way that they would travel in order to spread the good news of Jesus to other cities. What Jesus said may come as a shock to most of us, but it is important that we understand the truth, which is being spoken here. While it may have a specific context in this portion of scripture, it is important for us to recognize the truth that is ringing true to us thousands of years later.

> Whatever town or village you enter, search there for some worthy person and stay at their house until you leave. As you enter the home, give it your greeting. If the home is deserving, let your peace rest on it; if it is not, let your peace return to you. If anyone will not welcome you or listen to your words, leave that home or town and shake the dust off your feet. Truly I tell you, it will be more bearable for Sodom and Gomorrah on the day of judgment than for that town. (Matthew 10:11–15)

In this portion of scripture, Jesus told His disciples to dust off the dust of the ground from their feet. While this may be in a physical sense, the implications are clear based on the last part of Jesus's directions. When He explained that it would be more bearable for Sodom and Gomorrah than that city on the day of judgment, it is clear that Jesus was saying that the city had received their chance to change. If they had not determined to accept it, that was their responsibility, and they would be held accountable for their actions. Now, what does this mean for a person in a mentally and emotionally abusive relationship? The truth is that most survivors have attempted to restore their relationship with their abusers because victims will always return to their abusers. With that in mind, you must understand that the goal of Jesus's disciples and that of survivors are often the exact same. The desire is to see restoration, one between God and man, the other between survivor and abuser. However, since the abuser sees no reason to change or accept responsibility for their poor behaviors, this makes reconciliation impossible. With this in mind, it should be noted that if reconciliation is impossible, we have the same instructions that Jesus gave His disciples. Brush off the dust of the ground. The dust is a symbol of former things, which have clung onto a person. If that dust was associated with rejection, then there is room for it to be shaken off by the one that has been rejected. However, it should be noted what exactly this means and what it does not mean. This is not an invitation for vengeance or an opportunity for the victim to seek anything other than freedom from mental and emotional abuse. This does not mean rejoicing when something bad befalls the abuser, but it also does not mean rejoicing with them in their victories. This is an invitation to a clean slate, which can only be found in becoming indifferent to the narcissist and becoming comfortable with living your life apart from them.

First, as was previously mentioned, this is not an opportunity or invitation to allow the abuser to continue to be part of our lives. In many cases, it is best to go zero contact with the abuser when possible. If, however, there are children involved, or there is some other extenuating circumstance, which prevents zero contact, the victim should remain wary and give it the best attempt they can at going gray rock. What happens at the beginning of the separation process from a narcissistic person is that the abuser will undoubtedly and without fail attempt to destroy the other person. The reason for this is that the abuser cannot be the bad person in the relationship. They also refuse to take responsibility for their actions, thereby placing all the responsibility on the victim, who was completely unaware of the extenuating circumstances, which were befalling them in the first place. However, eventually, the narcissistic person will stop attacking and possibly even recant the attacks they've placed against their victim. Ever playing the victim, the abuser then leaves out key details about what had happened in the relationship, which caused the breakdown of it. Only smearing the name of the victim and presenting themselves as a helpless victim are the motives of the narcissist.

Upon recanting, however, the hopeful victim will often fully forgive and attempt to make the relationship work, despite the fact that the abusive person has not truly changed. This is a very sad state of affairs because the abused victim believes that their abuser truly sees what they have done wrong and has a desire to change it. Due to this, the victim will return to the abuser or will desire to still have their abuser be a part of their lives in hopes of change and restoration. In this instance, the survivor will naturally wish good upon their abuser because the victim still desires to see their abuser become everything they had promised or even told the victim that they were. The victim desires only to see good come to the person, who is the object of their affection, because the victim is still very much so in love with the abuser. This is natural, and every normal individual will only want to wish good on the person that they love. This is a natural reaction for the victim in love. However, this is where the rubber must meet the road for the victim. Determining that how they were treated was not okay and that they will never allow themselves to be devalued in that way ever again is a powerful stance, which takes time for the victim to come to. Please remember to be patient with this process. Every person operates at a different speed of healing. However, remember that the journey is just as important as the end result and the things which you are learning in the process will prove to be valuable tools, which you can carry with you for the rest of your life.

The moment that a person stops wishing well on their abuser is a moment filled with all sorts of different emotions. The most intense emotion, however, is most likely the emotion of anger. This emotion, which is natural, can then cause the victim to do the opposite of wishing good on their abuser and will begin to spiral into a stream of anger in which they only wish bad upon their abuser because above all else, the victim desires justice to be served. Unfortunately, in many cases, the victim will never truly see justice served to their abuser. This leaves the victim feeling helpless and angry, unable to change the situation they find themselves in yet unable to see justice be served to the person who has so wrongfully treated them. This anger then reels the victim into thoughts and ideas of wishing bad upon their abuser and wishing for justice to be served. Friend, please do not take the bait of allowing yourself to live a life of bitterness. When the survivor of narcissistic abuse chooses to live life wishing the worst upon their abuser, there is no true freedom to walk in. The victim remains in a state of the victim mentality and is unable to walk out the call that God has for them. The purpose for this book and the reason you began reading it was to experience freedom from your narcissist and the control that they have over you. Seeking vengeance and wishing bad upon them is not going to lead you to freedom. True freedom only comes from choosing to move on with your life without the presence of the narcissist in it. There will come a moment in time where the victim will choose to recognize the truth of the relationship that they find themselves now free of.

As has been mentioned previously, the person that you believed you loved did not truly exist. There was always a piece of themselves which they kept from you, and they were not truly the person they claimed to be. In the most intense cases of narcissism, it is quite possible that the person was the polar opposite of which they sold to you. The person that you believed you loved did not truly exist. They were simply a mask, which was used to cover the darker parts of your narcissist. This truth can cause a person to become even angrier because they begin to wonder how they could have been so foolish to believe this lying and manipulative person over people in their lives that truly cared about them. Unfortunately, this is the nature of the narcissist. They are master manipulators and every-thing comes back to the idea of being in control of their victim. Read that again. Everything comes back to the idea of being in control of their victim. Everything comes back to the idea of control. What if a victim were to determine that they would no longer be controlled by their abuser? Therein lies the key to freedom from the anger you are experiencing. The game of relationships to a narcissist is one of control. Should a victim decide to take a stand and no longer allow their abuser to control them, then perhaps there is a form of justice. It may not be found by the outside world, but it can allow inner peace for the victim, who is choosing to become a survivor. The justice comes in the victim, knowing the truth of who and what their abuser truly is and determining that since the difference between who the abuser claimed to be and who they truly are is so different, the abuser no longer means *anything* to the victim. The person who the abuser pretended to be may have meant something to the victim, but the person the narcissist truly is does not. Therefore, how can the victim be angry with a person who they are only just now meeting? They can no more be angry with the false persona that their narcissist put on than they could be angry with a Halloween mask that their child put on while making poor choices.

However, now that the victim can see the true person behind the mask, they have a choice to make about this person that they are seemingly meeting for the first time. The victim must determine whether they want this new person to be a part of their lives or do not. However, based upon the terrible actions, which come with a separation from the narcissistic person, as well as the devaluation process, which takes place inside of the relationship, the victim should find the strength to honor and respect themselves enough to determine that they have no desire for a person like this to be a part of their lives. This then leads the survivor to the point of determining that rather than wish good or bad upon their narcissist, they will choose to simply not wish on them at all. This way of not wishing on their abuser at all is a step, which could be known as indifference.

Becoming indifferent to a narcissist will take time and space. This is the reason so many people will highly recommend zero contact in a broken relationship with a narcissistic person. The distance allows the victim more clarity daily into who the person truly is that they have recently broken away from. The victim may begin doing things that they enjoy again and, even more importantly, begin discovering the things that they enjoy again. With a little distance and a little bit of truth, the victim will begin to feel human again. This is a beautiful feeling, and eventually, there will be days where the victim doesn't even think about their abuser. You are probably thinking that seems impossible. However, it is the beauty of taking time alone with God and hearing the truth about what you have just experienced, as well as the truth about who you really are. Once again, this indifference does not mean that the victim chooses not to forgive the narcissistic abuser for what they have done to them. Choosing not to forgive their abuser would only allow the abuser more power, and the survivor would lock themselves into another prison of control to their abuser. Rather, the victim must choose to forgive and release. That is to say, they must choose to move forward with their lives without the presence of the narcissistic individual. The idea of shaking the dust off your feet rings clearly and truly here because the victim has the opportunity to shake off the dust of the lies and pain of an abusive past relationship and begin to move on with their lives. The reality is that this is more freedom than the survivor has had in a very long time because they are able to make a choice for themselves that will benefit them and allow them to walk into the call that God has for their lives.

What does it look like to move on with your life without your abuser? The answer is simple: You become indifferent to every aspect of them in your life. This means you do not check up on them. In some cases, you may even block their numbers or social media. This means that their opinion of you does not matter to you. This means that you do not care whether you see them or you don't, and in most cases, you would prefer not to. This means you do not pray for them. This means you do not care whether things in their life are going bad or well. In short, you simply do not care what happens to them or about them.

I'm sure that more than a handful of people will take issue with what they have just read. It may seem like hatred or anger, but it is not. It may sound dark and cold, but it is not. Once again, who your narcissist truly was, was a total stranger to you. So to not care about a total stranger would not be dark and cold. It would simply mean that you were living your life, and you had not developed any type of relationship with that stranger. Think of all the people you pass by when you purchase groceries. You don't wish bad on those people. You don't wish good on those people. You simply do not wish on those people at all. You are indifferent to those people, and it is okay for you to become indifferent to the person who has used and abused you as well. Most of the strangers you meet from day to day have probably never done wrong by you or abused you in any way. Yet we act with indifference toward them and do not feel negatively about it. Why then would becoming indifferent to a person who has abused you hold negative connotations? Jesus Himself told His disciples to shake off the dust of their feet as a sign against them. Well, as a survivor, you aren't wanting a sign against your abuser. You are simply wanting the dust off your feet. You want to be free and done with your abuser, and you deserve it. Whether people around you understand it or not, this is your freedom cry. What you have stayed awake crying and praying for God to take away from you, the intense pain, which the abuser caused you, was paid for by Jesus on the cross. It's okay not to understand it, but do not push away the very help which God is attempting to send you. In Jesus's time, all the Jewish people were expecting and anticipating a Messiah, which would come to rage war against the Roman Empire and give the Jews freedom on a physical plain. However, in most cases, God's way of redemption and freedom will look very different from ours. We discussed the anger and desire for justice that can entrap victims earlier in this chapter. What if justice is in fact coming, it just looks a little bit different than what we had expected? What if, rather than justice looking like the abuser getting karma, it looks more like the survivor becoming indifferent to their abuser and thereby taking back their power from their abusers? Taking back their power means a great deal of things for the survivor of a narcissistic relationship. This means that the survivor now has power to make decisions, to stop negative thought processes, to recognize truth, and choose to believe what is true about them rather than what one person has told them about themselves. This is not simply a cry of resentment and anger, rather it is a battle cry of freedom, which comes in the form of the word *indifference.* Sometimes being indifferent may look different based on circumstances. But indifference holds one fundamental truth, and it is tethered to your freedom.

In conclusion, this chapter has touched base on some basic information on how to handle your narcissistic abuser moving forward. This will allow for you to begin living your own life once again and valuing and respecting yourself the way that you always deserved. The first step is recognizing that how you were treated was not okay and choosing to take steps toward developing quality relationships with quality people that will treat you with respect hereon. This step can lead victims to desire to forgive their abusers and act as though nothing has happened. However, if a survivor truly respects themselves, they will recognize that the way they were treated was not okay and will not allow for that type of treatment ever again. This then will cause the survivor to move into a stage of anger in the healing process, where they desire to see justice served and will want to see their abuser get what they have coming. However, living with this idea of justice being served and desiring vengeance only places the survivor into a cage, where the abuser still has the rights to call the shots. This then ultimately leads to the victim discovering the truth about narcissistic relationships, and it is all about the abuser receiving and maintaining power over the victim. Upon further introspection, the victim will discover that the person that the narcissist claimed to be was only a mask and will then begin to realize that the narcissist themselves means absolutely nothing to the survivor. This then brings the survivor to the one place where true freedom can be received, and that is the place of becoming indifferent to their abuser. Once again, becoming indifferent does not mean that the victim does not choose to forgive the narcissist, but rather they choose to forgive and then move forward with their lives without the presence of their abuser. Once the survivor reaches this state of indifference, true freedom has truly begun because the victim has chosen to become a survivor and no longer live in a state of victimhood. This is a great step toward freedom, but there will be many battles and struggles. For this reason, it is important for the survivor to know and recognize who their true enemy is, and that is the truth we will uncover in the next chapter.

CHAPTER 9

The Real Enemy of My Freedom

It is common that the victims of narcissistic abuse tend to view the narcissist as their enemy. The truth, however, is quite different. Rather than viewing our lives from a physical perspective, at this point, it is imperative that we begin to look at our lives through the eyes of God. It's important to understand that what has been attacked is so much more than just your mental and emotional well-being. Your very self-worth and how you view yourself has been completely destroyed based on the devaluation you have experienced through your narcissist. However, this is a plan that goes far beyond an individual wanting to destroy you. It goes to the very level of spiritual warfare. What we have experienced up to this point is the understanding of what has happened on a physical plain. However, if we are to truly heal and then begin to walk out our freedom in the way of fulfilling God's call on our lives, we must look deeper. And in order to do so, we must begin to understand who our true enemy is, and we will discover that through the help of the word of God.

First of all, we have to understand that we are not fighting against our narcissist. This may seem counterintuitive to healing; however, it is rather foundational. The Bible tells us, "For our struggle is not against flesh and blood, but against the rulers, against the authorities, against the powers of this dark world and against the spiritual forces of evil in the heavenly realms" (Ephesians 6:12).

Recognizing that while your narcissist may have been the tool, which your true enemy used to manipulate and attempt to destroy you as an individual, that there was something far more sinister behind the scenes, is truly freeing and empowering. No longer do you fixate on your narcissist and desire justice to be served, rather you set your eyes on your true enemy, who is here with one purpose only, and that is to destroy you as an individual. Your enemy knows that if he can destroy your reputation and/or your morality, he is then capable of derailing God's plan for your life. The truth is that the moment you surrendered your life over to Jesus, you became a huge threat to your enemy. The enemy that we are discussing here is of course Satan.

The Bible references him as a dark and malevolent being. The Bible says to "be alert and of sober mind. Your enemy the devil prowls around like a roaring lion looking for someone to devour" (1 Peter 5:8).

If our enemy is truly out hunting like a lion, then it stands to reason that we must be something worth going after or hunting down. In the grand scheme of things, the enemy is less interested in disrupting your physical well-being and is more interested in taking you out of commission in building the kingdom of heaven! The old adage goes, "If the devil can't make you sin, then he will make you lazy," in other words, keep you from using your gifts that God has given to you for destroying the kingdom of darkness and usher in the kingdom of light. His tactics have not changed, and our enemy is still out to destroy you. Again, he is less interested in destroying your physical well-being or what makes you comfortable in this life and more interested in getting you into a place of comfortability and complacency so that you will no longer be an effective tool inside the kingdom of God. This is the reason why, for the person still pursuing purpose in pain, that the enemy will lead you to believe that it is best to let the painful parts of your life pass by. Don't forgive, and don't forget. Hold on to the bitterness and pain so that it will never happen to you again. This may appear to be the same as being indifferent, but it is not. Because forgiveness is a part of being indifferent. You choose to become indifferent to the person as a whole, and this includes the past, present, and future of that person. The enemy knows that if he can get you to use a majority of your bandwidth on your abuser, then it does not leave much room for you to operate in your gifts and therefore to be effective for the kingdom of heaven. Herein lies what the enemy is after and what he has always been after in the history of humanity.

Let's trace all the way back to the garden of Eden. God has finally created the crowning piece of His creation in human beings. God appears to be almost infatuated with these seemingly meaningless creatures. And when they worship Him, God appears to value it even more than when the angels sing His praises. This begins circulating around heaven, and eventually, Lucifer catches wind of it. Now it should be noted that Satan was God's leading worship leader in heaven. This just became another reason for Lucifer to despise God and desire to be "like the Most High." From this point, Satan plans and leads a rebellion against God in which one-third of the angels of heaven determine to follow Lucifer as well. They were cast out of heaven, and Satan was given a place to rule that was the opposite of paradise. However, ever the schemer, Satan then determined to cause separation between man and God. This came in the form of Adam and Eve, giving into temptation and committing the first sin in the garden of Eden. Whether it was at the beginning of time or today, Satan does not have any new tricks. His plan and goal are always the same, and that is to remove our authority and capability to make an impact on the world. Adam and Eve, in the very beginning, were given dominion over everything. They had authority over everything on earth. And through manipulation and deception, the enemy took that authority from them. Those two terms, *manipulation* and *deception*, should sound very familiar because they are the tools which the narcissist uses regularly. The narcissist will manipulate the victim into believing what they want them to believe. Manipulation is one of the most powerful tools of the narcissist because it is in manipulation that the victim's views of reality begin to be changed and warped. However, the narcissist is not the one that is out to destroy the victim or at least not on their own. One of the greatest deceptions that we can fall victim to as survivors of narcissistic abuse is the lie that our true enemy is the narcissist. This is a tactic of the enemy, which allows him to continue running rampant in our lives because our minds become so enthralled with the negative actions of the narcissist that we get our eyes off our true enemy. In a lot of ways, the enemy uses the narcissist as a decoy so that he can come in and ransack our lives in every area of our lives. The enemy knows that if he can keep our eyes off him and what he is attempting to accomplish, then he will be left free.

> The thief comes only to steal and kill and destroy; I have come that they may have life, and have it to the full. (John 10:10)

Let's unpack that verse for a second. It is vital to move on to understand that our enemy is not the narcissist but rather the power that is behind and is driving the narcissist's poor behaviors. Now that we recognize the true enemy of our souls, what is he after? The answers can be found right here in this portion of scripture. He wants to steal, kill, and destroy. But what does he want to steal, kill, and destroy? The answers to these questions are simple: He wants to steal your authority, which was given to man all the way back at the beginning of creation.

> And God blessed them, and God said unto them, Be fruitful, and multiply, and replenish the earth, and subdue it: and have dominion over the fish of the sea, and over the fowl of the air, and over every living thing that moveth upon the earth. (Genesis 1:28)

When Satan first deceived Adam and Eve, he took away their authority of all that God had given them. It was only when Jesus died on the cross that our authority was truly restored, and it can only be given to us through a personal relationship with Jesus. We now have authority over every attack that the enemy might come against us with, and we have authority to resist the temptations, which he may try to use against us! In other words, we have the authority to live our lives how we desire to, which, for those of us who truly love God, is to live a holy lifestyle. For those who do not have a personal relationship with Jesus, however, it is not possible to live a life free from sin and bondage.

Not only does the enemy want to steal your authority or, in other words, power or control, but he also desires to kill the vision that God has given you for your life. It is so true that once you stop dreaming of what you wish your life to look like that you begin to lose hope. Losing hope for something that only God could do is the beginning stages of death because we know that the truth of Jesus's death and resurrection is a true story of hope. Hope is what the foundation of our relationships with God is based upon. If we do not believe or have hope in the call of God on our lives, then it is a vision that may never come to pass. The Bible tells us that "where there is no vision, the people perish" (Proverbs 29:18).

The hope of Jesus within us should drive us to desire to share the good news of Jesus to all those around us! It should burn inside us like a wildfire, being revealed to all around us through unique gifts, which God gave us for the purpose of bringing others to Him! If there is one thing that the enemy would want to make sure never sees the light of day, it would be your unique call and gifts, which God has always intended for us to use as tools to bring the kingdom of God here! At this point, it would be wrong for me not to mention that the enemy also has a plan for our lives. If he cannot keep us from living for God, then he will, at the bare minimum, make us useless for the kingdom of God!

The enemy wants to steal our authority. He wants to kill the vision that God has for our lives, but he also wants to destroy the kingdom of God. There is nothing more in this world that scares our true enemy like a Christian that is operating in their gifts and calling. That said, the enemy will do his best to keep you from being effective in building the kingdom of God. In some cases, he will create so much opposition in a person's heart or mind that the person begins to operate under the power of the enemy. This can look a lot of different ways. But in the case of the narcissist, they certainly utilize several of the tools, which the enemy also used throughout history, and the reality is that hurt or hurting people do in fact hurt other people. It is a sad truth, but most people who suffer from NPD are actually suffering themselves from past trauma, which they have never allowed to be healed by Jesus. Additionally, every one of these individuals also had a unique call, which God had created for them to accomplish. However, with them having allowed themselves to be manipulated by the enemy, they have forgotten the call of God in their lives. This can often lead to envy and frustration toward those that are following the call of God for their lives, which in turn causes the narcissist to begin to attack others that are seeking God's will for their lives. These attacks are sent by our true enemy as he attacks the insecurities of the narcissist. Now, not only are those suffering from NPD not building the kingdom of God, but now they have actually begun to work against it as they attack the calls that others have on their lives. For our true enemy, this is a brilliant strategy. Talk about compounding the interest on your investment! For this reason, we must never lose sight of our true enemy. In every case, we know that our true enemy is Satan, and his ultimate goal is to destroy the kingdom of heaven. However, the good news is that the enemy's attacks will not prevail.

> And I tell you, you are Peter, and on this
> rock I will build my church, and the gates of hell
> shall not prevail against it. (Matthew 16:18)

The manipulative thoughts and lies, gaslighting, and deception, which the narcissist seems to use so very effectively, are not born in the mind of the narcissist themselves, but rather it is birthed by the father of all lies. In many ways, we see parts of our true enemy within the narcissist. However, it is important for us to remember that the narcissist is also still a human and therefore the pinnacle of God's creation with all of the same potential within them to help make the world a better place. Unfortunately, they have allowed our enemy to manipulate them to such a degree that rather than being an effective tool that can be used for building the kingdom of God, they have become a weapon of destruction for the kingdom of darkness. However, it is important to remember that the battle we are waging is not in the physical realm. The Bible says, "For we do not wrestle against flesh and blood, but against principalities, against powers, against the rulers of [a]the darkness of this age, against spiritual hosts of wickedness in the heavenly places" (Ephesians 6:12).

Rather than retaliating and attacking a person who is being controlled and manipulated by the enemy, why not begin directing our prayers and spiritual warfare against our true enemy? His desire is to get to use your narcissist as the ultimate scapegoat, while he continues to ransack your life. However, what if he also is using you? For as you begin to take the fight to your narcissistic abuser, you are being used to attack another human being as well, someone that, just like you, was placed at the very pinnacle of God's creation. This makes you no better than your narcissist. Choosing to forgive, even when poor behaviors continue, can be tricky, but know that you can still have boundaries in place. Forgiving a person does not necessarily mean granting them access into your life. Forgiveness and trust are not synonymous with each other. Particularly when the same behavior patterns, which have been forgiven, continue, we must remember, however, that the narcissist is not our true enemy but rather someone that has been lied to and manipulated by our true enemy into helping build the kingdom of darkness unknowingly. For so long, they have believed the lie of the enemy that they themselves are worthless, and so they believe that in breaking down and destroying others, they actually better themselves. This of course is all a narrow-minded and feeble attempt to make the narcissist feel whole, but it does not and will not help because, as we have mentioned before, the narcissist is not secure in themselves as an individual. They have no idea of their identity in Christ and therefore continue to operate as powerless victims when they should be acting as powerful overcomers. This is just a clear revelation of the words of Jesus when He tells us, "Do not be deceived: God cannot be mocked. A man reaps what he sows" (Galatians 6:7).

Since the narcissist has not taken the time to invest in their relationship with God and discover who they are and who God is to them, they will only reap the lies of the enemy, which will in turn bare bad spiritual fruit. How sad is this recurring pattern of the narcissist? Without a true encounter with Jesus, the narcissist will remain in their former way of living, which never leads to joy or contentment. This then begs the question, How do we keep ourselves from traveling down the same road as our narcissistic abuser? How do we move on with life and fulfill the call that God has placed on our lives in spite of the lies of the narcissist? The answer lies within the path that brought the narcissist to the place of becoming like the father of all lies, and we will discover the answers to these questions in the next chapter.

CHAPTER 10

You Come Forth!

Moving past narcissistic abuse is not an easy task. Many people will find themselves doubting the truth and gaslighting themselves for months and potentially even years after leaving the narcissistic relationship. However, rest assured, there is hope. Something good can in fact come from all this that you, as a survivor, have experienced. It is time for you to begin to recognize and call out the greatness that still lives inside of you! For far too long, you have been locked away. Buried underneath the lies that the enemy has told you. There is still greatness that the world is waiting to see! Just because you have been devalued by one person does not mean that you do not still have value. Odds are that you feel the odds are stacked against you because, as previously mentioned, the narcissist will go out of their way to ensure that they create every opportunity to destroy you, which includes creating flying monkeys among other ways of manipulating those that are in your sphere of influence. However, rest assured that no matter who sees you in the twisted light, which the narcissist has contrived, you still have support, and more specifically, you have an audience of one. The one person whose opinion matters in all this is your Heavenly Fathers, and He still views you as perfect in His sight! He still sees greatness! He still has a plan for your life, and it is time for you to begin to walk in it!

In a lot of ways, being in a narcissistic relationship is like death. This was the person that you fell so deeply in love with so quickly.

This was the person that you thought you would spend the rest of your life with. This was the person that you were willing to go through hell or high water for. So once all these things have been promised, and you've lived up to your part of the agreement, it's no wonder that you feel so very hurt and betrayed, why you feel like a part of you has died, and in some ways, you even fight for the strength to carry on. There, however, is beauty in all this, which you will discover in time as we discover with Mary and Martha in this portion of scripture:

> "Lord," Martha said to Jesus, "if you had been here, my brother would not have died. But I know that even now God will give you whatever you ask." Jesus said to her, "Your brother will rise again." Martha answered, "I know he will rise again in the resurrection at the last day." Jesus said to her, "I am the resurrection and the life. The one who believes in me will live, even though they die; and whoever lives by believing in me will never die. Do you believe this?" "Yes, Lord," she replied, "I believe that you are the Messiah, the Son of God, who is to come into the world." (John 11:21–27)

To everyone around, it appears that Lazarus was dead, never to be seen or heard from again. And in so many ways, this is what we experience post–narcissistic relationships. We begin to wonder how life can possibly go on and whether we could ever fulfill any type of purpose with our lives. After all, the one purpose we had in filling a person's narcissistic supply, we have failed at. This, however, is an impossibility for anyone to fill. Without a true encounter with Jesus, the narcissist will remain a bottomless pit of need for supply. While the victim continually attempts to fill the needs of their narcissistic counterpart, they slowly start to lose pieces of themselves until they are simply a robot, performing tasks to appease the narcissist. The victim begins to loathe themselves because they recognize their inability to make the narcissist happy, no matter what they may try. The victim is left in a daze and slowly buries every piece of themselves in an attempt to protect themselves and make themselves more desirable to their abuser. The crazy thing about this entire interchange is that the narcissist is not our actual enemy. While the narcissist may intentionally use and abuse their victims, that is not the endgame of our true enemy. Our true enemy is the devil, and his true objective in all this is to ensure that you do not be used for helping to build the kingdom of God. The enemy's end goal is to take you out of commission. If he cannot make you give up your faith in God, then he will, at the bare minimum, make it so that you are not bringing others to come to know Christ!

If there was one other reason for this book to be written, then it was this: to make you aware of your enemy's attack in your call to be an effective warrior in the kingdom of God. We are called to go and make disciples, yet so many of us have been silenced by the lies and attacks of both the narcissist and the enemy in our lives. When will this stop? When will we, as sons and daughters of God, determine to believe the truth of God's words to us over the lies of our enemy? We have been told that we are dead and have been placed in a spiritual and emotional tomb, but Jesus is on the way. When Jesus enters into your situation and makes Himself real to you, rest assured that everything changes! Everything changes because you have someone that comes alongside you and says that He does not see you as dead but rather as alive and thriving with potential. You have someone that comes in and breathes fresh life into your dreams and the call that He has placed on your life! You have someone that shouts into the grave and calls out your greatness by name, shouting for it to come forth!

There are so many pieces of you that you have changed in order to become more attractive or desirable to your narcissistic counterpart. But the beauty is that it only takes one momentary encounter with Jesus for it all to change. One moment of hope is where you recognize that while your narcissist may have attempted to play god with you, they are in fact not God, and therefore, you need only look in the right place to discover your true value and how much you are truly worth. Nothing about you has changed since you've been in the relationship with your abuser. You've simply buried everything that made you uniquely you. When you begin to allow that person to resurface, you will begin to discover that not only is their greatness inside of you but that you are truly a good person. Being able to go to sleep at night and know that you are a good person who has done the best that they possibly can do is worth everything because it means that you have peace in your mind and your heart. Again, with gaslighting, being an ever-present threat to the victim of narcissistic abuse, peace in your mind and heart can be very difficult to achieve. Once you are out of the realm of a narcissistic relationship, you can look back and see where you were led to question things that were said and where your personal opinions or feelings were discredited. The truth is that you, like any other human being, are entitled to your feelings and opinions. When you felt poorly about something your narcissist said to you or a way that they treated you, it was not a bad thing for you to voice how you were feeling. This basic communication is something that was silenced by your narcissist, and in doing so, they took the first step in silencing who you are as a person. However, looking back at the old relationship, you can now see where your feelings were undermined, and you were treated poorly. This is where you can begin to be reborn! To be able to voice or express your feelings or emotions is a powerful tool! We see, continuing on in this portion of scripture, that Jesus did this as well!

Jesus wept! (John 14:35)

Now it may just be me, but if Jesus felt free to express His feelings in regard to a situation that made Him feel negatively, then I feel that we should be able to express ours as well. When we do, there is power that is released because we can release and stop focusing on the negative feelings that we have experienced and can truly focus on the task in front of us! Jesus stopped and wept, but He did not stop there. This shows that Jesus was not simply complaining about His negative situation, but rather, He intended to change His circumstance through action! Entirely, too many people get stuck here. They spend the rest of their lives living in the grave, complaining about what has happened to them rather than determining to take action and allow their pain to be the catalyst to their unique and beautiful call to change! The first step is to of course turn to Jesus, but then we must also express our pain to Him and express our need and desire for Him to take it away. Jesus does not want to be brought into your pain. Jesus wants to heal your pain! Much like a good doctor, Jesus can only heal what we are open, honest, and vulnerable about.

Ironically, the only way to begin the healing process is by choosing to forgive the person that harmed you. In doing so, you choose to recognize that no matter what they may do, they could never possibly make up to you what they've done. However, rather than harboring bitterness and rage toward that person, you choose to release them from what they owe you. This often can come in the form of many tears, and this step will likely have to be repeated. When we choose to forgive, we are removing the chains or grave clothes that so strongly tie us down to where we are. When we allow dead things to sit, they rot. This can cause our outlook on life and to live in the freedom that God has given to us to stink. Choosing unforgiveness will cause our lives to resemble what many of the people in Lazarus's town believed about him.

> Jesus, once more deeply moved, came to the tomb. It was a cave with a stone laid across the entrance. "Take away the stone," he said. "But, Lord," said Martha, the sister of the dead man, "by this time there is a bad odor, for he has been there four days." Then Jesus said, "Did I not tell you that if you believe, you will see the glory of God?" (John 11:38–40)

Without clean hearts that desire to serve God, our vision will be skewed and without direction. The moment that we confess our pain and choose to release the person that has done so much harm to us, we then have the freedom and opportunity to hear the voice of Jesus! Oftentimes, in the hustle and crunch of trying to please the narcissistic person in our lives, we can drown out the voice of God. As one old adage goes, "If the devil cannot make you sin, then he will make you busy." You now have the opportunity after voicing and working through your emotions to hear the voice of Jesus calling out to you! For far too long, you have allowed yourself to be in your mental and emotional tomb. It is in this moment that Jesus can begin to express to you who you are to Him, and in doing so, He gives you a divine call and destiny that He desires to see you fulfill with your life! The only question is, will you choose to stay in the tomb as so many do, beneath the debris of mental and emotional pain, broken promises, and unforgiveness, or will you choose to rise up and walk back into the unique and divine calling that God has placed on your life? The voice of Jesus is calling the greatness that you once showed out of the grave and back to life! Not only does God want you to be able to live a happy and healthy life, He also desires for you to be a part of His army, which wages war on and plunders your one true enemy. I'm sure there have been points at which you have wanted vengeance and to see retribution for the things that your narcissist did to you. But remember, they are not your true enemy. Your true enemy is the enemy of your soul, and he desires to see you never fulfill the call that God has placed on your life! What better way for justice to be served than for you, as a warrior in the kingdom of God, to begin to move forward and obliterate the kingdom of darkness. Satan set out to destroy you; now Jesus is giving you fresh eyes to see your true enemy, and He is giving you an opportunity to be a part of your true enemy's undoing.

Choosing to focus on what is ahead of us allows us to have hope. When we choose hope, we cannot help but become individuals that share our hope with others. Every single person has unique gifts and abilities, which Jesus desires us to use to help in the building of His kingdom! Our enemy would have us believe lies that we are not capable or worthy of being a part of such an amazing army, and unfortunately, he will often use other people to do it. The truth, however, is very different from what we've been told. Not only are we capable of being a part of this army that goes and sets captives free, but we are handpicked by God. Just imagine, there is not a single person on this earth that has been placed in the exact same situation as you. God has placed you exactly where you are at, at this exact time, around the exact people you are around, doing exactly what you are supposed to be doing, for a purpose. You have been handpicked, and you have everything that you need to be fully effective in building the kingdom of God. Now if God is that intentional with where He placed His warriors, don't you think that your enemy will also be strategic? This did not only come down to your enemy attacking your ego, the enemy was out to take you out of commission so that you would not be effective in helping to build the kingdom of God.

Now that we know the tactics of our enemy and recognize what must be done in order for us to reestablish our lives, there is only one thing left to do: It is time for you to take a stand in your mind and determine to respond to the voice of Jesus, just as Lazarus did.

> So they took away the stone. Then Jesus looked up and said, "Father, I thank you that you have heard me. I knew that you always hear me, but I said this for the benefit of the people standing here, that they may believe that you sent me." When he had said this, Jesus called in a loud voice, "Lazarus, come out!" The dead man came out, his hands and feet wrapped with strips of linen, and a cloth around his face. Jesus said to them, "Take off the grave clothes and let him go." (John 11:41–44)

God has so many great things in store for you and a great plan that He intends for you to fulfill with your life. Rather than looking back and regretting the outcomes of what has happened in the past, it is time for you to look forward to the future and walk out of the grave of despair! It is time for you to pick up the weapon that God has entrusted you with and begin to do battle with the enemy! You are not worthless. You are needed, and you *are* loved beyond understanding! It is time for you to focus on the love of Jesus and get your eyes off the pain and devastation of your past! It is time for you to respond to the loving call of your heavenly King! Hear Him as He cries out in love, "(fill in your name), come forth!" The invitation has been presented. It has been long, dark, lonely, and painful along this journey, and this is by no means the end but rather the beginning to your healing process. The truth is that you can move from victim to survivor, but it depends upon how you choose to look at the abuse that you've been set free from. Is your mindset that of a victim or a survivor? Victims choose to live in the pain of their past. Survivors recognize the pain and allow themselves to adapt and grow from the pain of their past. So which one will you be? Will you be the person that allows your narcissistic abuser to continue to control you through head games, or will you be the person who chooses to respond to the loving voice of Jesus and come out of the grave of mental and emotional abuse? The choice is up to you. The battle lines have been drawn. Your true enemy does not want you to fulfill your call and live out a fulfilling life in which you fulfill God's purpose for your life. So what will it be? Will you allow yourself to be defeated before the war has even begun, or will you stand and fight alongside the One Who loves you beyond all imagining? The call is yours, and freedom is only a stone roll away.

"*You* come forth!"

ABOUT THE AUTHOR

Ryan O'Connell was born on July 20, 1990, to Stephen and Debbie O'Connell in Danville, Illinois. He was raised here, and the little Midwest town has a special place in his heart. Ryan is a single father to his two sons, Izrael and Ezra O'Connell, and believes that God has a plan in mind for his future. In addition to writing, Ryan also has founded a business by the name of My Mental Revival. Ryan enjoys spending time with friends and family and loves attending the Vineyard Church in Urbana, Illinois, every Sunday.

9 798889 309215